COLLINS *Essential Guides*

Curriculum Co-ordinators in Primary Schools

Mick Waters

Acknowledgements

I would like to thank some people who were directly or indirectly
involved in the development of this book:
Helen Nicholls, a teacher in Plymouth, for her help with Chapters 5
and 6.
Sue Lacey, Sally Young, Parmjit Paddan, Dave Waterworth, Diane
Hunt, teachers from Sandwell LEA and Anne Teague and Christine
Smith, two teachers from Lancashire, who have allowed the use of
their examples.
Kathryn Forsyth, Clive Carroll, John Peatfield and Clive Davies, who
all work in the In-service Department at Lancaster University and
have offered ideas and suggestions.

Published by Collins Educational
An imprint of HarperCollins*Publishers*
77-85 Fulham Palace Road
Hammersmith
London W6 8JB

Reprinted 1997, 1998

ISBN 0 00 3177203

Designed by Chi Leung
Printed by Martins The Printers, Berwick upon Tweed

Contents

FPS 14076
£7.99 BM
011

Introduction

Did you jump or were you pushed? Did you look for greatness or did you have it thrust upon you? Did you choose to be a co-ordinator or were you asked, selected, or required to take on the role?

For some teachers, the chance to act as the co-ordinator for a curriculum subject is exciting and professionally fulfilling. The role represents a step on the career path which, if done well, may lead to further responsibility within the school or elsewhere. The post may carry with it a small rise in salary as a recognition of its demands.

For other teachers, the job of co-ordinator is yet one more pressure in their overcrowded professional life. They may be happy to oversee the subject, or they may take it on because someone has to, while their favourite subject is done by someone else. In small schools they may be responsible for co-ordinating several subjects with varying levels of knowledge and understanding. The co-ordinator may be the head as well as a class teacher. The role of a co-ordinator in primary schools is so various that it is almost impossible to find a typical example.

What is typical is that co-ordinators have a demanding and difficult task which has many facets requiring a great range of skills. People try, often without preparation, to do the best they can for the school, for colleagues and for the children. The problem of time is enormous.

This book offers support for the co-ordinator. It offers ways of thinking through the challenges of the job. It suggests ways of getting started and strategies for meeting demands. Suggestions are made for working with colleagues or others. Examples are offered which, with a little adaptation, could offer short cuts and ways through problems.

This book is aimed mainly at subject co-ordinators and the examples and documentation are drawn from subject co-ordination. However, the principles and approaches covered are applicable to all co-ordinators. Equally, teachers with a management role in Scotland will find the book of relevance, even though the documentation used is different.

After reading and using this book the job will still be demanding and challenging. For those who sought the challenge it is a treasure map to be explored and enjoyed. For those who were pushed it is a branch to cling on to. For everyone, I hope it will be of benefit to teachers and to children in the classroom.

Defining the job

The job of the co-ordinator is complicated and has changed and developed greatly over the years. Initially the co-ordinator's role was that of a supporter; today co-ordinators are managers and while expectations in some schools are trivial, in others they are daunting.

Curriculum managers

The *Primary Matters* document produced by OFSTED in 1994 talks of curriculum managers who have specific and considerable responsibilities:

- Developing a clear view of the subject
- Providing advice and documentation
- Organising teaching and resources.

For the first time it was recognised that if such tasks were to be undertaken then time needed to be made available 'during the teaching day'.

Expectations

Since *The Primary Survey* carried out by HMI in 1978, the job has changed from modelling desired behaviours and attitudes into leadership, strategy, deployment and negotiation, a much more daunting and strenuous task. To emphasise the responsibilities associated with the role, recent OFSTED inspections on individual schools give some of the expectations:

'There are co-ordinators for most subjects of the curriculum and for aspects of the work of the school, such as special educational needs and base-line assessment. The allocation of these responsibilities is in need of review since some teachers have more than they can effectively carry out. Following a re-allocation, subject **co-ordinators should be given a greater role in implementing and monitoring a balanced programme of work in their subject. If they are to do this effectively, they will need some non-contact time.**'

'The school now needs to **review its existing practice and agree a consistent approach** which addresses all aspects of English in the National Curriculum and supports a balance within the subject. The co-ordinator's role is crucial in leading and developing the process.'

'The role of curriculum co-ordinators is not sufficiently well defined and some of the senior staff carry too many responsibilities and their workload is consequently too heavy. **The staff needs to work more coherently on a whole school basis**, thus harnessing the talents of individuals.'

from OFSTED *reports on individual schools, 1995*

Curriculum co-ordinators: the job

The Leeds Primary Needs Project gave the first definitive agenda for primary curriculum co-ordinators, as this summary shows:

- Convert programmes of study into policy statement/curriculum guidelines/schemes of work for their own school. This will need to be done in consultation with colleagues in their own and linked schools.
- Be prepared to advise and support colleagues both when advice and support are requested, and equally important, when it is needed.

- Manage the resources including:
  - budget management
  - development of resource centres
  - deployment and use of resources.
- Monitor, evaluate, assess, record, report.

- Be an exemplar:
  - looking to own teaching contribution
  - working alongside colleagues
  - organising seminars/workshops
  - developing in-depth knowledge
  - overall curriculum/how children learn
  - resources available
  - appropriate National Curriculum targets
  - appropriate National Curriculum Programmes of Study
  - assessment arrangements.

The role of the co-ordinator - where are you?

One way of looking at where you are uses a model developed by Berkshire LEA (*see page 7*). Instead of expecting everything to be done at once, it recommends looking at where the individual co-ordinator is, and then sees the process as one of working out from there and building a set of school roles. A useful analogy is that of dropping a pebble in a pond and letting the ripples move out.

Stage 1: Getting started as a new co-ordinator
At the centre are aspects which can be developed in the teacher's own classroom using gentle persuasion. These are low-key jobs which are only slightly more demanding than previous work.

The role of the co-ordinator

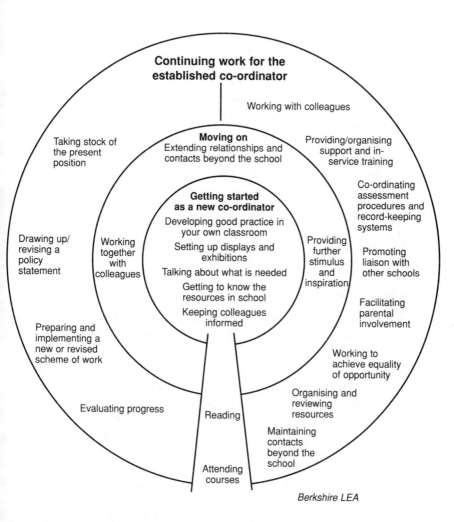

Continuing work for the established co-ordinator

Working with colleagues

Taking stock of the present position

Moving on
Extending relationships and contacts beyond the school

Providing/organising support and in-service training

Co-ordinating assessment procedures and record-keeping systems

Getting started as a new co-ordinator
Developing good practice in your own classroom

Setting up displays and exhibitions

Talking about what is needed

Getting to know the resources in school

Keeping colleagues informed

Drawing up/revising a policy statement

Working together with colleagues

Providing further stimulus and inspiration

Promoting liaison with other schools

Preparing and implementing a new or revised scheme of work

Facilitating parental involvement

Working to achieve equality of opportunity

Evaluating progress

Reading

Organising and reviewing resources

Maintaining contacts beyond the school

Attending courses

Berkshire LEA

Stage 2: Moving on
This means moving out and trying to extend the work.

Stage 3: Continuing work as an established co-ordinator
In the outside circle the established co-ordinator can start to work for more extensive influence and much more strategic management.

At all stages it is necessary to read, attend courses and build up a professional knowledge of the subject area.

Summary: What we know about co-ordinators

Research, OFSTED reports and information from co-ordinators show some key points about the job:

1 Co-ordinators have a crucial role to play in school development planning.
2 The effectiveness of co-ordinators often rests upon personal qualities and standing rather than simple status.
3 Lack of time is a major problem for effective co-ordinators.
4 Co-ordinators often feel ambivalent about their role, not always able to direct or enforce their ideas.
5 Many co-ordinators feel they were not equipped for their role before starting.
6 The curriculum focus is still largely subject-based but recently more appointments have been made for areas such as assessment or teaching and learning approaches.
7 Co-ordinators are able to influence continuity and consistency throughout the school, if given the opportunity.
8 A classroom teacher's confidence can be greatly enhanced by the work of co-ordinators.
9 The job of the co-ordinator is too vast to do all at once.
10 Co-ordinators need clear roles and responsibilities.

Clarify your role

One way forward is to seize on point 10 above and to look at how well responsibilities are negotiated with the senior management of the school.

Most curriculum co-ordinators will have *a job description*. Your job description outlines the range of tasks. It is usually very general and descriptive but states the sorts of responsibilities which might be reasonable for someone who is in charge of a subject area.

Following this a co-ordinator needs *a job specification*. This outlines the types of tasks the co-ordinator will be expected to undertake. Words like 'maintain' show the upkeep aspects of the job, such as monitoring resources and keeping systems in order. Words like 'promote' show developments that are expected to take place. The IT co-ordinator may be expected to promote links between IT and other curriculum areas. Words like 'ensure' might highlight some of the things that have to take place within the subject, such as ensuring children with special needs are identified and catered for.

Also useful is *a job focus*. This helps to identify and define *short-term targets* and it structures the use of time over the immediate future, perhaps two or three terms. A job focus helps to prioritise activity so that the co-ordinator and other members of staff know which aspects of the job are paramount at that moment for that person.

The National Curriculum and OFSTED criteria

Understanding the subject

Knowing the fundamentals of the subject is essential. Without this knowledge, policy documents and schemes of work are difficult to devise, support is hard to offer and resources are hard to supply. The National Curriculum spells out the child's entitlement and expectations of content and OFSTED publications provide a useful background to the criteria for good practice in the subject.

Using the documentation

A useful way to get to know and understand the demands of the subject is to explore available documentation using the OFSTED inspection criteria for quality of learning in schools. When inspectors enquire into the quality of learning they work in seven areas:

1 Learning environment
What are the features of the learning environment for the subject, including aspects of teaching, that will help pupils to learn effectively?
2 Pupil learning experiences
How will the subject be presented to pupils so that they learn it most effectively?
3 Resources
What resources are appropriate and how will they be managed?
4 Curriculum and assessment
Is the curriculum organised in a way which ensures pupil entitlement and progress?
5 Teaching
Is teaching effective? Do teachers manage the work of children in the most effective way?
6 Partnership with parents and the community
How are parents and others involved in the children's learning?
7 Cross-curricular links
How does the subject link with others and contribute to the wider issues of the child development?
8 Management
How is the subject overseen and developed?

These are hard questions for the co-ordinator to answer, particularly if you do not see the subject as a personal strength or specialism. You must therefore look for clues, and there are some significant starting points.

Establishing criteria

To establish criteria for quality in the subject you will need:

1 The National Curriculum requirements for the subject.
2 *Guidance on the Inspection of Nursery and Primary Schools* (HMSO, 1995).
3 The OFSTED book for your subject entitled *The implementation of the curricular requirements of the Education Reform Act.*
4 A selection of four recent OFSTED inspection reports on individual schools. These can be obtained from HMSO, free of charge.
5 The recently published document about inspections for your subject entitled *A review of inspection findings (OFSTED).*
6 Any LEA guidelines or support booklets for the subject.
7 A blank chart on which to make notes *(see page 11).*
8 About three hours.

Read the documents listed above and gradually get clues about each section of the criteria that inspectors use. As issues become apparent, jot them down. You will see trends emerging, issues being developed in different places and the same patterns coming through.

Prompts to support the development of criteria for quality

Learning environment
- display
- play equipment
- safety procedures
- fieldwork

Resources
- range and quality
- progression
- pupils use of
- accessibility
- library provision/use

Teaching
- expectations
- methods
- organisational strategies
- use of time
- homework

Cross-curricular links
- Social, moral, spiritual, cultural (SMSC)
- use of IT
- citizenship
- economic awareness
- equal opportunities

Pupils' learning experiences
- collaborative working
- personal study
- respect for other people's feelings
- setting own task
- development of self esteem
- learning skills

Curriculum and assessment
- coverage
- provision for SEN
- continuity and progression
- assessment procedures
- marking
- agreed procedures
- use in planning

Partnership with parents/community
- contribution to pupils' learning

Management of subject area
- monitoring/evaluating
- support
- identification of relevant priorities
- development work
- financial planning

Guidelines to promote quality in ART

Learning environment
- Bright and stimulating display which reflects other cultures and traditions - to include artists and craftspeople within the children's own work - equal opportunities.
- Learning environment which promotes visual investigation.
- Safety procedures - children taught in accordance with health and safety requirements.
- Fieldwork - links with community, visits to local galleries and areas of interest - parental involvement.

Pupils' learning experiences
- Pupils reflect on and adapt their work in the light of what they intended and consider what they develop in future work.
- Express ideas and opinions - pupils given opportunity to talk about and reflect on their achievements.
- Show interest in their work and their contributions to life in the community.
- Appreciate other traditions, cultures and feelings.
- Pupils need to be allowed to make their own interpretations and make informed choices of media.

Resources
- Easy access for staff and children - clearly labelled.
- Range and quality - across all six areas.
- Library provision - staff and children.
- Progression.

Curriculum and assessment
- Assessment needs to: identify various levels of understanding and skills; reinforce and extend pupils' skills in investigating and making, together with their knowledge and understanding.
- SEN - art activities raise self-esteem. Pupils should not be deprived of creative experience for academic support.
- Pupils' work needs assessing constructively.
- Agreed school policy for assessment and marking. Assessment used to inform curriculum planning.

Teaching
- Homework - gathering of background information.
- Work independently, groups, whole class, pupil explanations and demonstrations.
- Structured activities providing opportunities for written, oral and research tasks. Direct instruction about nature and history of art.
- Skills, knowledge and understanding need to be developed.
- Expectations - appreciating the child's own work and individuality.

Partnership with parents/community
- Non-teaching assistants need to be fully briefed to support pupils effectively (rather than over-directing).
- Informing parents of attainments through reports etc.
-
-

Cross-curricular links
- IT, cameras, computer software, OHPs, photocopier, video. (SMSC-citizenship, equal opportunities)
- Pupils should be introduced to work of a variety of craftspeople and artists to develop appreciation of diverse cultural heritage; selection to include the locality - past, present, variety of cultures.

Management of subject area
- Using artists in residence to enhance enthusism and help achieve a high standard.
- Using development plans to develop plans and identify relevant priorities and targets and evaluate progress - teaching and curriculum development are monitored, evaluated and supported.

Guidelines to promote quality in DESIGN & TECHNOLOGY   *Key Stage 2*

Learning environment
■ Children should recognise hazards and teachers should instil in pupils the need to work safely at all times.
■ Areas should be large enough to ensure the practical nature of the subject can be accommodated.
■
■

Pupils' learning experiences
■ Pupils should consistently use and extend their knowledge, understanding and skills as they design and make products.
■ They should use an increasing range of techniques, processes and resources.
■ Children should have the opportunity to work individually and as part of a team.
■

Resources
■ Equipment should be well maintained and accessible to pupils (in areas that are labelled, organised).
■ Consumable items should be monitored to ensure that projects can be completed.
■
■

Curriculum and assessment
■ Assessment criteria should be integral to the planning of schemes of work.
■ They should be integrated successfully into teaching and learning in lessons.
■
■

Guidelines to promote quality in PHYSICAL EDUCATION   *Key Stage 1 and 2*

Teaching
■ Support knowledge and understanding of the subject.
■ Structure work so that it is challenging, progressive and attainable for all pupils.
■ Lesson planning - differentiation, development, time management.
■ Involve children in self-evaluation, and of others, and in refining and improving their performance.

Partnership with parents/community
■ Reporting to parents.
■ After-school activities - transporting pupils to matches.
■ Links with Sports Development Unit/ Sports Clubs/sponsorship.
■ Sports Days/Activity Days.

Cross-curricular links
■ Be aware of cultural differences in dress and changing facilities.
■ Use different aspects of dance to enrich children's language and knowledge of cultures. Use dance in assemblies.
■ OAA - links with maths/geography.
■ PE - links with Health Education, (PSE), maths.
■ Positive attitudes, following rules.

Management of subject area
■ Monitoring subject - ensure progression and development.
■ Supporting staff - INSET.
■ Prioritise criteria for effective management of subject.
■ Budget for resources - maintenance and effectiveness of equipment.
■ Ensure coverage of National Curriculum.

At the end of three hours you will have a real picture of the demands of the subject. By reading, re-reading, flicking backwards and forwards through the documents, comparing one with the other, seeing the same issue from different angles, you will become familiar with the subject. You will gain confidence in knowing the subject criteria. It is time well spent. Some examples of completed charts are given on pages 11-12. If several co-ordinators need to be doing this exercise at once, there is a real focus for a staff in-service closure day where everyone is involved in a structured review of criteria for quality in subjects.

Towards a school teaching and learning policy

Once the criteria are established they can be applied.

1 On looking through the issues that emerge and teasing out the central ones, a set of important points becomes apparent. These become the principles that will guide the teaching of the subject.
2 Clear clues will have emerged about what is poor practice. As you establish the principles you might also state the practice that will be detrimental to learning in the subject (*see below*).
3 If the criteria for different subjects are put together, the co-ordinators can compare the issues that are emerging and tease out criteria that are:
   • specific to the subject
   • the same for another or several subjects
   • the same for all subjects.
Those that are the same for all subjects become the core of a teaching and learning policy for the school and do not need rewriting for every subject. Look at the example of principles below and consider which apply to all subjects and which are subject specific.

Four fundamental principles in the teaching of MUSIC

Positive
• Children taking responsibility for decision making in music - planning, exploring, editing, making, presenting, analysing, monitoring, evaluating.
• Children actively involved in music making through a variety of roles, individually and in groups - composer, performer, director, in audience, in analysis.
• Children are able to contribute and have an understanding of their own music making and the music making of others within class, school, amateur, professional, which is appropriate to their individual needs, interests, abilities and expectations.
• Children having opportunities to develop appropriate effective qualities in and through music, awareness of the senses - aesthetic awareness.

Negative
• Mass sing-songs behind the piano without focus/purpose.
• Music appreciation sessions i.e. writing about composers.
• Music as background.
• Listening to music without a focus/purpose.
• Projects on composers/instruments of the orchestra.

Curriculum monitoring

Monitoring and evaluation can be confusing and worrying; many co-ordinators are unsure of what the terms mean and how they are supposed to go about this part of their job.

- *Monitoring and evaluation* comprise the routine collection, organisation and analysis of factual data, to allow judgements to be made about future curriculum development.

Monitoring and evaluation are part of a process of curriculum development. To think what the co-ordinator's job might be, it is often sensible to ask straight questions. So for monitoring, ask 'How well are we doing?' To answer this, you will need to go through a process that looks at various aspects of the work of your subject.

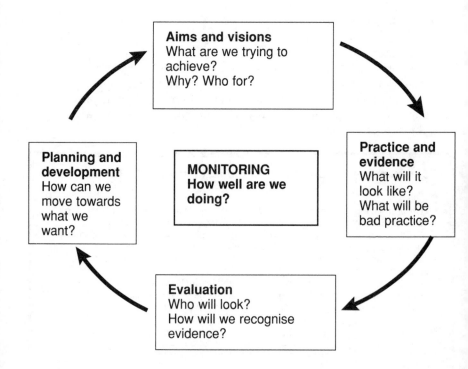

Aims and visions
What are we trying to achieve?
Why? Who for?

Practice and evidence
What will it look like?
What will be bad practice?

MONITORING
How well are we doing?

Planning and development
How can we move towards what we want?

Evaluation
Who will look?
How will we recognise evidence?

A good starting point is to consider issues from the work done on understanding subject criteria (*see page 10*). If you know what is meant by quality in certain areas, then through monitoring you can audit quality. It may be useful to look carefully at:

- Learning environment
- Pupils' learning experiences
- Resources.

Curriculum monitoring is a key element of curriculum leadership. It should be overt, supportive and developmental. It should extend understanding of the subject area and its teaching. Good curriculum monitoring begins with the audit·and review of practice and should highlight good practice as well as problems. Monitoring and evaluating are part of the process of development planning. If each co-ordinator plans the development of their subject and the plans are put together for the whole school, a School Development Plan emerges. Producing a subject development plan is dealt with in Chapter 12 (*see page 68*) This chapter and Chapter 4 (*see page 22*) will prepare the ground for your subject plan.

Strategies for monitoring

People are often unsure of how to go about monitoring the curriculum and think they have to do it entirely by themselves. However, there are many ways of looking at the practice of the school which involve several people and give lots of important and valuable evidence about the work being done.

1 Mutual observation by pairs
Two teachers agree to observe each other teaching and then discuss what they have seen. This exercise will provide a lot of information for each teacher and make them both think about their work in the classroom. Watching someone else is one of the best ways to look at yourself.

2 Observation by headteacher/deputy or curriculum co-ordinator
If you really want to look at the quality of, say, mathematics teaching in school then you need to spend some time observing in the classroom. The head, deputy or co-ordinator is ideally placed to look at issues such as continuity, progression and differentiation throughout the school and it is part of their responsibility to see teaching in action.

3 'Talk through' a classroom visit
Observation is one thing but shared understanding is another - much can be learned from encouraging teachers to talk through the way in which they organise their classrooms. Some schools have regular staff meetings in different classrooms where the teacher who is hosting the meeting talks through the way in which their classroom is managed. This should not be onerous or threatening; it takes only a few minutes

but it provides opportunities for all teachers to monitor practice throughout the school.

4 Samples of pupils' work
Pieces of work could be collected from each class. The aim is not to score points or to prove that one teacher is generating a level of achievement that others are not, but simply to see the range, scope and quality of work being developed.

5 Moderation of children's work
Schools have become very skilled at moderating work due to the impact of assessment procedures over the last few years. The very process of moderating throws light on monitoring and evaluation issues in school and generates information for the co-ordinator.

6 Talking with pupils
Talking with children about the teaching and learning they receive can shed light on many issues to do with classroom organisation and curriculum expertise. It is important to listen. The perceptions of the learner can be very illuminating. Questioning can be formal or informal; if informal, it must be a constant and developing process rather than a one-off conversation.

7 INSET days, exchange of staff, visiting other classrooms
In-service days can be used to implement many of the strategies already mentioned, and can also provide opportunities for visiting other teacher's classrooms and talking in depth about practice. They can also be used for exchanging staff between schools or departments.

8 Regular review sessions
Using a staff meeting to ask other teachers about aspects of the subject that they think need attention is a form of monitoring.

9 Discussions within joint planning sessions or at the end of jointly planned work
During a planning session or at the end of recently completed work, discuss the strengths and weaknesses within the curriculum area. It will give co-ordinators much food for thought.

10 Parents' comments
Whether given formally or informally, parents' comments can be used to shed light on matters of concern to them within the teaching of the subject.

All these strategies are ways of monitoring the curriculum but sometimes they will not be practicable. The curriculum co-ordinator needs to see what is going on through do-it-yourself monitoring.

Do-it-yourself monitoring

Collect work from different classes
Collect two examples of 'average' children's work from each class and put it in year order on the floor.
- Does it tell you anything about the development of aspects of the subject?
- What does it tell you about progression?
- What does it tell you about the development of skills?
- What does it tell you about children's expectations?

Take photographs
During one term take a selection of photographs and then study them.
- What are they saying about the 'range' of work in the school?
- What are they telling you about the finished work that children produce or the stages that they go through in their work?
- What do they tell you about storage systems or resources?

Count resources and books
You could do an audit of resources.
- Is the appropriate equipment in the right place?
- Is there enough to do the job properly?
- Does the range meet all ability levels?
- Does the equipment work?
- Are there sufficient books to cover the subject area for all age and ability levels?
- Are they attractively presented and accessible?

Ask children questions
Structured questionnaires will give a sample of pupil opinion and perceptions within the subject.
- Do they like mathematics?
- Do they understand the need for fieldwork in geography?
- Do they feel challenged in PE?
- What do they think of the writing they are asked to do?

The results are revealing for staff and interesting to children, and they may give pointers to the co-ordinator.

Survey parent or teacher opinion
Just as teachers gather information from children by asking questions, so you might use other sources, e.g. parents or other teachers.

Curriculum strolling
Walk around the school looking for evidence that your subject is being given prominence. It could be displays, book collections, a group of artefacts, chalkboard work, children's books, resources ... anything.
If you do a curriculum stroll every three weeks or so and make a few

notes, you will quickly build up a picture of the prominence or otherwise of the subject.
- Does the impact of the subject change?
- Is there a difference in emphasis between infants and juniors?
- Is the subject prominent in some classes but not in others?
- Are there examples of coherence between subjects?

Study displays
Visit the displays in school.
- Is your subject well represented?
- Is there emphasis on all aspects of the subject?
- Does the display cover a range of curriculum content?
- Are children dealing with the subject knowledge or does the display push them into processes and understandings?
- Are displays about finished products or developing ideas?
- Do the displays ask questions?
- Do the displays demonstrate progression through the subject or link with other subjects?
- What messages do the displays give about what is important in the subject?

All of these are methods of collecting evidence about your subject. It is worth thinking about ways to structure the monitoring of the subject; it cannot all be done at once. If you have time in the school day to do some monitoring then use it well. You only need a few minutes now and then if you have planned what you are looking for in your subject.

Monitoring is about asking straightforward questions

The examples on pages 20-21 show how a co-ordinator can spend a little time usefully by planning to audit the quality of work. A chart is used to prompt thinking about the following questions:
- What will I look at? (Aspect of the subject)
- What should I see? (Criteria for quality)
- How will I collect information? (Audit method)
and then after the audit asking:
- What have I found out? (Evidence)
- What are the issues that emerge? (This is part of the evaluation.)

The Creating Action Plans chart helps to keep thinking on track and limit the range of things to be audited and monitored; it acts as a focus for thinking. Study the completed charts and see whether you can follow the thinking. You can see what was selected as a focus and how the co-ordinator planned to find out what was happening. In the third column you will see what was found. At the end of the process, issues are identified for action. Some are urgent and need attention; some are more long-term; some are for the co-ordinator and some are for others; some are worrying and some are positive. It is easy to think of monitoring as finding fault. It is not, it is a process of finding out the state of the subject and ensuring that it is done properly. You should find some good news.

Using good news - letting people know

When co-ordinators look at the work of a school they often find that it is very successful. Schools need to develop ways of informing people of strengths and achievements. There are many people who need to be informed:

1 Parents

How do you tell parents what the school is achieving and what the children can do? You could use newsletters. It is not unusual now for the electricity board to tell us that 95 per cent of call-outs were dealt with within three hours. How about telling parents that 95 per cent of the children can read at the level expected for their age?

2 Governors

If governors are to represent the school, they need to know what the situation is, and teachers need to tell them. Is there a part of every governors' meeting which is designated to a review of particular curriculum areas?

3 LEA

For LEA schools it is important that advisers and inspectors know about some of the quality work that is being achieved. All too often the LEA only hears about problems and difficulties.

4 OFSTED

Schools are more likely to give a good account of themselves and do well in inspections if they can show that they have been self-monitoring quality and achievement in their school.

5 Secondary schools

A primary school may be in partnership with several secondaries; if it is able to demonstrate the children's achievements and abilities, those pupils will have the best opportunities for effective learning when they get there.

6 Teachers

If teachers in school know what has been achieved, their expectations are likely to be more realistic. Too often expectations are low because teachers do not understand what can be demanded.

7 Children

The children in the school need to know that their work is of a high standard or that their behaviour is good. Some graphs, charts or tables suitably organised for younger children might be a good way to demonstrate progress. Photographs, letters of thanks, log books and reports are all ways to show good news to children, and if they can be involved in collecting the data, so much the better.

ART

Creating action plans: Audit phase

Aspect	Criteria for quality	Audit method	Evidence	Issues
What will I look at?	*What should I see? Specifically*	*How will I collect information?*	*What I found out*	
The learning environment Whole group/individual teaching.	• Variation in teaching methods. • Group activities. • Individual learning activities.	• Talk to colleagues. • Visit classes when there is non-contact time. • Look at planning.	• They say there is a balance. • No class teaching observed. • No mention of styles.	• Little variety of teaching style. Lots of individual work. • No group work. • Raise issue to staff.
Pupils' learning experiences Providing works of art to influence the children's work.	• Examples of work by artists of importance. • Special attention: to topical works of art to project, i.e. Impressionists.	• Talk to colleagues. • Chat to children while working. • Discuss styles and topical situations.	• Needs to be more accessible. • Art co-ordinator solely in charge of providing each class with works of art.	• Staff do not know works of art. • Little enthusiasm in some staff.
Providing displays of children's work.	• Encouraging good standard of display: cross-curricular, across key stages.	• Collate art and design items during term for displays and records of achievement.	• Most classrooms offer stimulating displays of a cross-curricular blend.	• Need of discussion with children about their environment. • More input from children rather than staff related.
Resources Usage by teachers and children that reflects progression and continuity. Colour mixing.	• Reception: Colour recognition. Work with individual primary colours. • Years 1/2: Colour mixing to secondary colours. • Years 3/4: Tonal work and extension of colour mixing process. • Years 5/6: Black, white, greys, shades and tones.	• Talking to colleagues about use of materials etc. • See that relevant materials are available in all classes across key stages. • Collect examples for portfolio.	• Displays in KS1 well presented. • Teachers and children making good use of resources and materials. • Concern about Y4/5.	• Tell others. • Teachers and children unsure of colour mixing. • Skills-resourcing poor.

HISTORY

Creating action plans: Audit phase

Aspect	Criteria for quality	Audit method	Evidence	Issues
What will I look at?	*What should I see? Specifically*	*How will I collect information?*	*What I found out*	
Resources Organisation/storage.	• Clearly labelled boxes/shelves. • Constant checking resources are returned to central store. • Awareness of new materials for all staff and how to use. • Easily accessible.	• Ask colleagues if they are able to find materials needed. • Get older children to use - can they? • Make sure room is not locked.	• Are aware resources are central (but one colleague unsure where to put single copies of books). • Soon gets untidy! • Maps and posters have no organisation or catalogue.	• History 'rolling' topics relate also to science and geography on whole school development plan.
Usage by teachers and children that reflects progression and continuity.	• Topics covered in working document have KS1 and 2 materials. • 'Rolling topics' so all children experience with less repetition.	• Ask colleagues if they have sufficient resources. • Discuss working document and suggestions for improvement. • With reflection to whole school and their subject topics.	• All resources well used. • Resources generally returned to central store. • KS1: Keep Sunshine scheme in classroom, everything else in central store.	• Need INSET or staff meeting to show staff central store.

Moving forward: acting on audits

The monitoring and evaluation discussed in the previous chapter will have highlighted success and achievement but will almost certainly have revealed some issues to be addressed. Knowing what the issues are is one thing; knowing how to address them is another. A plan of campaign is required, a calculated look at how the practice in school can be developed to achieve what is expected by outside criteria and in-school aims.

The co-ordinator cannot do everything, neither are they responsible for everything: all teachers should have a commitment to the aims of the school and should share in making everything work in school. Delegating responsibility and authority does not mean giving it away, but dividing the workload while continuing to share the task. The co-ordinator can think through the whole school picture to plan where developments need to take place.

Addressing the issues

1 Where are we now?
The chart on page 23 shows the thinking of a geography co-ordinator grappling with the jobs that need doing in one school. It is useful to look at what needs to be done and, as well as deciding on priorities, to clarify who has the responsibility or the power to make things happen.

The Where Are We Now? chart is a thinking sheet, a prompt which helps to organise thought following an audit that has raised important issues. Try it for your curriculum area and see whether having a structure helps you to sort out your own thinking.

2 Creating Action Plans
Another example (*see page 24-25*) picks up directly from the Creating Action Plans chart used to prepare the monitoring of the curriculum area (*see pages 20-21*). The audit sheet (*see page 24*) identifies issues through the analysis of evidence gathered in school. It is then possible to continue the process (*see page 25*) and decide:

- What *action* needs to be taken?
- *Who* will take the action?
- By *when*?
- How will *success* be recognised?
- What *problems* can be envisaged and overcome?

Where are we now? The jobs that need to be done

	Needs attention and managing				Whose job?	OK and developing			
Budget	Future allowance for course attendance.	Co-ordinator needs to take part in KS1 geography lesson.	Time to discuss for curriculum monitoring.		SMT	Awareness of lack of resources.	Have been given time to discuss topic matrix.	Policy has been written.	List of resources has been written *but* not circulated.
Topic matrix/rolling programme.	Schemes of work.	Progression through school, e.g. locality work.	? Topic boxes *but* storage.		Co-ordinator	Building up sets of textbooks.	2 globes - one for each key stage.	Mapping skills.	
Awareness of existing resources.	Knowing storage of existing resources.	(KS2 teachers) Use of files as opposed to school boxes.		KS1 Use of atlases?	All teachers	Display.	Use of KS1 Sunshine.		
No specific resources for SEN children.	Need link with contrasting locality - KS1, KS2.				Outside support	Attendance at INSET offered.			
Writing reports.	Useful: comments in continual assessment.				All teachers				

Discuss which approach, e.g. (1) timetabled separate topic, (2) part of cross-curricular theme, (3) short term bursts, i.e. 3 weeks on Rivers.

ideas/ presentation by co-ordinator?

MATHS

Creating action plans: Audit phase

Aspect	Criteria for quality	Audit method	Evidence	Issues
What will I look at?	*What should I see? Specifically*	*How will I collect information?*	*What I found out*	
Pupils' learning experiences Differentiation in classes according to ability.	• Wide range of activities - group or individual. • Detailed planning - short term plans. • Flexible grouping in class.	• Visit classrooms - photograph examples of work and discuss with teacher. • Look at short term plans. • Visit classroom and discuss with teacher.	• No differentiation in year group in one class. All children doing same activity (extension activity available). • In one class some differentiation - a one-off lesson? • Detailed short term plans showing some differentiation. • In both classes children sit in age related groups but staff say there is some crossover where children work better at some subjects.	• Concept of differentiation needs to be discussed - difficulties of planning for different abilities over two-three age groups in one class. • Check regularly that plans and lessons match! • Visit classrooms again in the future.
Crossover between age groups in each class according to ability.	• Flexible grouping in class - across age groups. • • • Recognition of stage each child is at in a certain skill.	• Visit classrooms and discussion. • • • Discussion and talking to children. • Observation.	• I saw none but staff say there is occasionally. For some activities children are vertically grouped. • Groupings in my class change frequently for different activities. • Children in one class found tasks easy and moved on to extension tasks whilst others struggled. • Children in other class were confused and did not understand task - mismatch? Some Reception children work with Y1 and vice versa.	• Revisit classrooms. • • • Need to see more lessons to determine whether any action is necessary. • Extreme tact!

MATHS

Actions	Who/when/by	Evidence for success	Problems envisaged
Workshops, staff meetings when talking about new orders. Visiting speakers. Talk about own problems - tact. Asking for support next year? Maths scheme! Discussion.	Staff as whole. Outside agencies.	Tasks matched more accurately to children's abilities.	Acceptance by members of staff of problem and recognition of need to solve it.
INSET on differentiation. Support in classroom.	Local college/adviser. Next term.	Differentiation in planning. Pupils working in different groups in classroom maths.	Staff reluctance/worry.

25

Decisions can be recorded on the grid and the process, from monitoring through audit and evaluation, identification of issues to action, can be reviewed. The advantage of using a grid like this is that the process is talked through several times. It is worked on by the co-ordinator, preferably with the support of a colleague. Senior management can talk it through again and help with problems, practicalities, solutions and alternatives. The whole staff can be aware of the issues by looking at the grid and teasing out the messages within it. It takes time to do but it is economical in terms of writing and format. The boxes ensure that aspects are not left uncovered because the framework pushes the thinking along.

As you study the example on page 25, try to follow the thinking of the co-ordinator and the way she is trying to sort out the issues that have come to light during the audit. The Problems Envisaged section is a very important one, and there should never be a shortage of problems to envisage. Whatever development the co-ordinator wants to see, whatever the action, whoever it is to be done by and whenever it needs to be done, it is essential that the problems are recognised. Very few things work perfectly. There are reasons for the shortcomings revealed by the audit. These reasons will resurface as problems at a later stage, the stage of trying to put things right. Problems envisaged are easier to face, so spend a bit of time thinking about them and be prepared for them.

Some likely problems

Resources
Ideas, developments and new approaches often founder because of inadequate resources, and they can be very difficult to refloat. If resources are unavailable, old or worn out, the chances of success are greatly reduced. Some problems can be overcome through planning or improvisation but, for example, to enhance the effective use of calculators in mathematics, calculators are needed. Lack of resources is among the most frequently quoted reasons for failure of new initiatives in schools. Sometimes it is an excuse, a way of rationalising failure; more often it is reality.

Attitudes
Plan for problems whenever people are involved. Bad attitudes can arise for all sorts of reasons: jealousy, insecurity, laziness, petty-mindedness, arrogance. Some people are like that anyway, but sometimes trying to change things causes the attitudes. Getting colleagues to recognise the need to move forward can be the hardest part. They see no problem, they have no evidence, they cannot see what they are not doing and they do not know what is needed anyway. The grid on page 25 might help. Try talking it through with colleagues so that priorities can be identified, clarified and justified.

It is not just teachers who may present attitude problems. It could be the parents who do not want this 'new' education, or the cleaning staff for whom the new approach means more work. It could be the children who have become happy with the tedium of the traipse through the mathematics scheme and are challenged by having to think and solve problems practically.

Buildings

Everyone has problems with the layout, age and state of repair of the school buildings, the space available, storage, display facilities, outside facilities or lack of water in classrooms. These, plus others, could spoil the new development and progress in the subject. As with resources, you have to be clear whether the building is really the problem or a plausible excuse. There are problems everywhere, but things that seem insurmountable in some schools are overcome in others.

Documentation

Documentation can be cumbersome, boring and overwhelming, or alternatively too brief, unhelpful and frustrating. Striking the balance is difficult and for this reason documentation should be seen as a challenge.

Conflicting priorities

Schools can only do so much and many initiatives die because people cannot keep going. Energy runs out, people get confused. They cannot remember who had the priority, why they were doing it, when it had to be done by or whether they have done it. An emergency arises that seems more important than a mere priority.

Having established the actions that need to be taken, the co-ordinator needs the support of the school management. They can give status to the development and ensure that individuals are not overloaded.

Limited expertise

Asking people to do things is fine if they know how to do them. However, lack of expertise inhibits people so much that they will fail to try, rather than try and then fail. Search for expertise inside and outside school but use the expert, not to do things, but to help others to do them for themselves.

Parent perceptions

Parents are always hearing how bad schools are, so they are often wary of improvements. Some recent curriculum initiatives, such as IT, are appreciated but not really trusted by parents. They can see the arguments for children drafting as part of the writing process but this conflicts with an image of writing things first time with no mistakes. Parents know that calculators are part of the everyday world but they are still uneasy about their use in school.

Time

Schools are staffed at minimum rather than maximum levels. Co-ordinators usually teach a class and often have more than one subject to co-ordinate. The workload increases and is not necessarily directly related to the classroom. In this climate, the urge to try to develop yet more is not always to the fore. If you want people to spend time developing approaches, you have to show that the effort will reap rewards; you have to be able to demonstrate the value.

These problems are very real and several will threaten any plan. Being prepared, anticipating and addressing them is part of the task. It is sensible to make others, including senior management and staff involved in developments, aware of what lies ahead. People are more positive and prepared when difficulties are anticipated. The real challenge, however, is to solve the problems, perhaps by good documentation, an effective meeting, some in-service training or some help in other teachers' classrooms.

Whole school policy documents

After working out what is seen as good practice in your subject and linking it to effective teaching and learning within the classroom, then monitoring and evaluating aspects of work and considering how whole school approaches might develop (*see Chapters 2-4*), you are working towards a policy for the school. As a policy becomes established, write it down to produce a policy document.

Many co-ordinators are encouraged to produce documentation as the first stage of the job. A problem that often occurs is that the documentation becomes paper to be filed rather than policy to be practised. The real policy is the one taking place in the classrooms and the documentation should support, influence and develop the learning of the children. This chapter and Chapter 6 (*see page 33*) offer some advice for producing documentation that will make a difference.

What is a policy document?

- The policy document is a step towards a whole school approach.
- It states the agreed principles that guide teaching and learning.
- It is used as a starting point for developing the subject provision.
- It serves as a marker against which the work of the school can be measured.
- It clarifies practice and specifies the standpoint of the school within the possibilities available.
- It emphasises good and bad practice.
- It brings together subject expectations and quality classroom practice.
- It can help parents, governors or others understand the work of the school.

What are the principles?

The principles are simple statements that summarise the beliefs, aims and philosophy of the school with respect to the subject or aspect under discussion. Two examples are shown on page 30. They express the views of the teachers concerned on how children should achieve most in the subject. Principles carry messages for teachers about how they should provide for children's learning. At this stage they provide no answers. In fact, for many teachers a statement of principles offers problems and challenges. It is the scheme of work (*see Chapter 6*) that will bring the principles into the classroom. The policy document sets the expectations.

Some useful principles for ART

- Encourage the practical use of different materials and techniques to express ideas of what has been seen, remembered or imagined.
- Be able to review and modify work in the light of criticism.
- Acquire a knowledge of an artist and be able to apply that knowledge to their own work.
- Show knowledge of art history, stating cultures and traditions, including the work of influential artists.
- See art as a means of expression and communication, forging cross-curricular links with other subjects.

Some useful principles for SCIENCE

- Encourage curiosity in children about their environment through a practical approach.
- Organise activities, experiments and investigations so that children are able to communicate their work to others in a variety of ways.
- Ensure teacher and child assessments are used in a way which supports and encourages the child to extend and challenge his/her ideas and findings.
- Encourage a collaborative approach as well as children being able to work independently.
- Encourage open-mindedness so children interpret their findings critically and do not always expect a 'right answer'.

How to write a policy document

Policy documents are perhaps the most important pieces of evidence a co-ordinator ever creates or holds. They can be the difference between a whole school policy approach that ensures the best possible deal for children and a sporadic, hit and miss approach to education that no child should have to endure.

The role of the co-ordinator is crucial to the process of producing an effective policy document; the policy will only ever be as good as the team that wrote it. So it is up to you to build a team capable of producing an informed, manageable, user-friendly policy that will make a difference to the children in their classrooms.

When policy documents are written (after consultation with colleagues) and genuinely represent improved practice in schools, the quality of teaching and children's learning can only benefit. If policy documents are written in isolation and enforced on colleagues, the quality of teaching and learning is unlikely to change.

1 Consultation

Consultation is the key. Successful implementation of the policy document demands that staff:

- Agree it
- Contribute to it
- Evaluate it.

2 Aesthetics

Ultimately the staff must have ownership of the document. Therefore aesthetic issues are important. Think about the:

- Size
- Shape
- Content
- Design
- Quality of reproduction
- Writing style
- Audience (illustrations, diagrams).

3 Dynamic or doorstep?

Do you want to produce dynamic or doorstep documents?

Dynamic documents	**Doorstep documents**
Concise	Detailed
To the point	Offer lots of examples
Diagrammatic	Anecdotal
Give an overview	Give an in-depth picture
Aide mémoires:	Use concrete examples:
- mnemonics	- children's work
- colour	- extracts from schemes
- shape.	- tips for teachers.

To combine the best points of dynamic and doorstep documents, a dynamic policy statement can be written in punchy, user-friendly language. It should be backed up with an appendix full of examples for staff to dip into if they do not fully understand the overview created or want more information. Some of the more challenging or contentious issues generated by new policy-making can then be tackled, explained and examined in detail in the appendix.

Writing a policy

There is no one way of writing a policy. Each situation demands its own plan, depending on the needs of the group and the individual and on their philosophies. Lifting policies from other schools and adopting them as your own rarely works; ownership is achieved by people working together to iron out difficulties. However, many good policies have been created by colleagues sharing and explaining their ideas and adopting tried and tested formats.

A policy production plan

Co-ordinators in schools wishing to use a whole school approach could use some or all of the following ideas.

You will need:

1 An agreed structure for the policy.
2 A house style of vocabulary and phrases.
3 A common logo to denote ownership by the school.
4 An agreed typeface.
5 An agreement on colour coding of subjects.
6 A procedure for taking the policy to the governors for ratification.
7 On completion, a rolling programme of dates for consultation on the policy's implementation.
8 A date for consultation to change or amend the policy.
9 A date in the long-term planning of the school for an overall review.
10 Evidence to show how the policy works in practice.

The advantages of this are that:
- co-ordinators are not in competition with each other to produce something bigger, brighter and better than the last one.
- co-ordinators make the plan for the format together with all staff and then work the plan for each new policy. This is much quicker than trying to devise something totally original every time.
- staff within the school (and any new staff who arrive) do not waste time learning the layout of each policy.
- all the agencies of the school community can easily read and interpret how the school aims are manifested in whole school policy documents and through evidence of the policies in practice in the classrooms.

Writing successful policy documents is dependent on co-ordinators building a team who work collaboratively *as* a group rather than a team who work individually *in* a group.

Developing schemes of work

The precise set of agreements about expectations in the subject set out in the policy document can now be added to by developing a scheme of work *(see pages 34-35)*. This supplies the detail, organises the content and supports teachers who understand the policy but are unsure how they should move forward. The policy sets the destination and the route; the scheme of work is the map and timetable to stop us getting lost.

Developing a scheme of work is an ideal opportunity for co-ordinators to weave some magic into their educational provision for young children. For co-ordinators this means being prepared to stand up for a curriculum that has all that is expected in breadth, depth and continuity but is rich in excitement, discovery and new opportunities.

Do children in your school:
- Want to learn?
- Take pride in their achievements?
- Have a rigorous attitude to work?

If not, why not?

What can co-ordinators do?

The best way is through a scheme of work which will actually take policy into the classrooms where it meets the pupils. But co-ordinators and their teams need to be quite clear about what they are trying to achieve in creating a scheme of work.

What children have to know:
- their basic entitlement
- the National Curriculum.

What colleagues would like them to know:
- absolute essentials
- value-added opportunities
- optional extras.

How you would like them to come to know it:
- teaching strategies and styles
- spirals for learning thorough a key stage
- blocked units of work)   see *Curriculum Planning at*
- linked units of work   )   *Key Stages 1 and 2*
- dripped units of work)   (SCAA, *1995*)
- rich and varied experiences.

How you would you like them to remember it:
- written formats

Geography Outline Scheme of Work

This is an outline scheme of work or overview map of curriculum delivery. It sets out to show what each teacher should be teaching in each year group for the Autumn, Spring and Summer terms. The idea is that staff can see where they fit into the overall scheme of curriculum delivery. It aims to help staff take ownership of their parts of the curriculum and to demonstrate that which should have been covered before and after their time in each year group.

	Autumn	Spring	Summer
Year R/1	**FOOD/CELEBRATION** • Introduce world map, where food comes from and process of farm → factory → shop. • Observe the weather and discuss seasonal change. • Introduce simple geographical vocabulary. • Draw simple plans of objects. • Follow and use simple directional terms. • Talk about different uses of land for growing food - orchards, crops, etc. • Visit local supermarket.	**CARIBBEAN - locality overseas** • Introduction to another place: what's it like? • Compare to home, focusing on climate, homes, environment, similarity/difference. • Express views on the environment, building on geographical vocabulary. • Understanding of an island. • Make simple maps of an island showing land, sea, village. • Reinforcement of world map, locating Caribbean. • Introduction of globes.	**HOUSES AND HOMES - school locality** • Recognise main physical and human features (shops, houses, roads, etc) different types of housing. • Discuss different homes around the world. Why are they different? • Observe local area. • Make simple maps of routes. Use teacher made maps to plot on details. • Discuss different scales on maps. • Express likes and dislikes. • Suggest improvements. • Understanding 'place' in relation to Plymouth, Devon, England. UK map. • Observe weather and compare to Autumn term.
Year 2	**OUR SCHOOL - village study** • Study a village which contrasts with features of Thornbury and has an old school. • Compare the two places. Similarities, differences. • Make plans of the 2 schools with simple key. • Understanding of village. • Birds eye view of village showing features in correct place. • Undertake work to improve one aspect of school, e.g. garden. • Use N, S, E, W when moving around the school grounds. • Signpost maps.	**CHINA** • Revise world map and point out China. • Comparisons of food, homes, crops, climate. • Discuss population and scale.	**MOVEMENT** • Introduction of aerial photographs of local area and industrial estates. • Discuss different uses of land and how people have changed it. • Visit of planning officer. • Use OHP to enlarge map sections of local area. • Investigate journeys and revise UK map.
Year 3	**TAVISTOCK - contrasting UK locality** • Recognise main human features of a market town. • Compare to Thornbury and suggest reasons for differences. • Study original functions: importance of river and situation of town. • Maps of town area showing roads, shops, houses, etc. • Look at street maps of towns. • Discuss environmental change, e.g. bypass. • Signpost maps from key points, what can you see from ... • Weather studies using IT	**AFRICAN VILLAGE - contrasting locality in Africa** • Study a village in Africa of similar size to Thornbury with clear differences. • Compare: why is it different? • Develop understanding of the links between climate, food, growth, i.e. physical factors affect human activity. • Continue references to world maps. • Develop geographical vocabulary. • Scale of Africa. • Use of atlases.	**EGYPT** • Develop understanding of the importance of the River Nile. • Follow its route using atlases, where does it receive water from? • Introduction of river vocabulary, e.g. tributary, flow, source, sea. • Investigate local site conditions in school grounds - temperature and wind speed. • Compare weather in 2 contrasting places: why are there differences?

	Autumn	Spring	Summer
Year 4	**INVADERS/SETTLERS** • Understanding of relief, high and low points around school grounds. Relief maps. • Recognise points of reference on Map A (UK map). • Use rain gauges and measuring instruments in weather studies.	**BRAZIL - locality in S America** Recognise main physical features of a rainforest. Understand why it is like it is. Develop appropriate vocabulary. Use a variety of sources. Continued references to world map. Size/scale of Brazil. Rainforest is only part. Conflict of interest. Land use.	**SHIPS/SEAFARERS** • Revise river points and visit Plymbridge to undertake river study. • Investigate flow, speed, channel etc and look at second stage - gorge, boulders, erosion and relevant vocabulary. Use as reference for later river studies in Year 5. • Continue references to world maps - oceans, seas.
Year 5	**TUDORS** • Investigate the original function of Plymouth. Visit the Barbican. • Use OS maps of Plymouth area and street maps. • Develop vocabulary.	**JAPAN** • Compare with previous studies. • Explain level of development, compare to previous studies. • Investigate location of main cities (near coast, away from mountainous interior). • Reinforce islands and refer to world map.	**PLYMOUTH AS A PORT - local study** • Understand why Plymouth is a port - 3 rivers. • Physical and human features. • Visit Hoe, Tamar valley. • Make sketch maps and reinforce river parts. • Understand importance of River Tamar and economic activities. • Use 4 figure grid references in studies of Plymouth landmarks. • Discuss links with EU especially France. • Plot development of Plymouth since 1945. • Weather studies.
Year 6	**VICTORIANS**	**INDIA - locality in Asia** • Describe the general features of the country. • Investigate in detail the features of a village (homes, jobs, level of infrastructure). • Understanding of why: physical/human factors, including population. • Continue references to world map. • Compare daily life and explain differences using range of geographic vocabulary.	**DARTMOOR and topical study** • Describe main physical features and explain why few people there. • Use OS maps on visit to Dartmoor and in class during studies. • Understand the resources of the moor: granite, clay and as an amenity and why this leads to conflict. Topical study could be part of this work or another issue, e.g. famine, pollution, conservation, whaling.

From a co-ordinators point of view it helps to map which parts of the programmes of study each year group gets. It helps to think about:

• If areas should be revisited: (i) how often, (ii) when, (iii) where.
• If the curriculum area is balanced: (i) across the school, (ii) within a key stage, (iii) across the three terms in each year.

Geography expanded scheme of work

Here the outline scheme of work is expanded to show the detail of curriculum coverage in the subject. Each year group would have an expanded scheme of work presented in three terms.

	TUDORS	JAPAN	PLYMOUTH AS A PORT - local study
Year 5	• Investigate the original function of Plymouth. Visit the Barbican. • Use OS maps of Plymouth area and street maps. • Develop vocabulary.	• Compare with previous studies. • Explain level of development, compare to previous studies. • Investigate location of main cities (near coast, away from mountainous interior). • Reinforce islands and refer to world map.	• Understand why Plymouth is a port - 3 rivers. • Physical and human features. • Visit Hoe, Tamar valley. • Make sketch maps and reinforce river parts. • Understand importance of River Tamar and economic activities. • Use 4 figure grid references in studies of Plymouth landmarks. • Discuss links with EU especially France. • Plot development of Plymouth since 1945. • Weather studies.

Detail for Autumn term

Term 1	Year 5	TUDORS
Element	**Knowledge and approaches**	**Skills**
Place	• Thematic study of Plymouth and its origins and settlement relating to Tudor period. Visit to the Barbican and harbour area. • Link to other places in Devon with similar functions.	• Use vocabulary: settlement, function.
Rivers	• Introduce children to River Plym. Look at location on OS maps in the classroom and mouth of river on location. • Use OS maps to find other settlements which have developed at wide river mouths in Devon, e.g. Dartmouth, Exmouth, Teignmouth, Sidmouth.	• Use relevant vocabulary: source, sea, harbour, inlet, port, mouth.
Weather		
Settlement	• On location describe main features of fieldwork settlement which help to describe features of the past, e.g. narrow streets, Tudor houses, proximity to water. Use evidence to deduce why settlement developed.	• Understand the importance of function in settlement origins. Offer explanations of settlement using maps and fieldwork evidence.
Environmental change		
Mapping	• Use a variety of maps to extract information about the original function and location of Plymouth. • Use of a street plan on location to orientate around Barbican. • Record features seen on visit on a street plan. • Use a map of Plymouth and highlight Tudor settlements. Keep map to add in another colour future developments in Term 3.	

Subject: **Science**   Separate: **Yes or No**

Science Outline Scheme of Work

It is worth spending time considering what the National Curriculum requires but also what you as a school want the children to achieve.

It is useful for teachers to know exactly what is expected from them in each term. It is important that teachers are therefore encouraged to read the detail of policies as well as the overview grids to avoid missing issues of importance in the delivery of a subject.

It is often helpful to teachers to see how many times an area of learning is revisited and where.

Where areas of the school have a designated purpose, it is sometimes necessary to provide a more specific diet. Additional guidance notes and procedures may therefore be needed.

	Year 1	Year 2	Year 3	Year 4	Year 5	Year 6
	Relevant PoS	Relevant PoS	Relevant PoS	Relevant PoS	Relevant PoS	Relevant PoS
Term 1	Ourselves; Light and sound	Changing materials; Earth and beyond	Grouping and classifying materials	Changing and separating materials	Electricity; Light and sound	Changing and separating materials
Term 2	Plants; Electricity	Animals; Forces and motion	Electricity; Light and sound	Animals: life processes and animals in the environment	Plants; Humans as organisms	Earth and beyond; Forces and motion
Term 3	Grouping and classifying materials	Forces and motion; Magnetism/Sc1 focus	Humans as organisms; Plants	Forces and motion; Earth and beyond	Grouping and classifying materials	Animals: life processes; Animals in the environment
Env. Studies						
Health Education						

Programme of Study Attainment Targets Attainment Levels Progression and Continuity

Y1, 3, 5: Plants
Y2, 4, 6: Animals

Humans as organisms

Check:

37

- display
- trips
- magical moments
- inspiration
- motivation.

But remember also that in the creation of a scheme of work every co-ordinator is putting together a package and therefore needs to:

1 Establish someone to oversee all the co-ordinators' efforts, pulling together all the working groups.
2 Avoid overloading the subject.
3 Establish a framework to work within.
4 Avoid prescribing schemes that inhibit staff.
5 Establish clarity and coherence when making planning decisions.
6 Avoid overcomplicating the curriculum.
7 Establish sound justification for decisions.
8 Avoid misinterpretation.
9 Establish whole staff agreement.
10 Avoid dissent.

Some practical pointers:
- **Grids** show clear thinking, are systematic and easily read.
- **Allocation of hours** shows expectation of delivery and manageability of the whole package.
- **Key words** help staff identify what is important.
- **Spirals** show staff how something builds up across a child's career, e.g. Christmas is different in every year group but makes a totally coherent experience over seven years.
- **A whole year plan** on one sheet is more easily absorbed.
- **A whole school map** shows staff where they fit in the overall scheme of things. They know what has been taught and what will be taught next.
- **A time audit** of available teaching time helps determine the timing of certain curriculum delivery, e.g. Harvest, Christmas, Easter, sports day, class assembly, school dentist, open days.
- **A list of suggested books and resources** provides support to individual teachers and saves time by relating available resources to learning aims.

Helping colleagues with subject ideas

One of the problems facing primary schools is whether to continue teaching through topic work. The demands of the curriculum and recent criticisms of the topic work approach have led many schools to review their curriculum plans and in some cases to reduce the scope of topic work in favour of a more subject-specific approach. Whichever approach is adopted, many teachers are aware that they lack knowledge in a particular subject area. Topic work seems to make a link between subjects for children but if the activities and tasks do not push children on in knowledge, skills or attitudes then there is little learning or progression. If each subject is taught on its own the same problem exists.

Many teachers need practical help and advice from the co-ordinator at the planning stage and on teaching skills in the classroom later. Co-ordinators are being used well when they are asked for help by colleagues. This is often incidental; sometimes co-ordinators only realise that help could have been made available some time after it was needed. The planning stage is the best time to offer support and makes the best use of a co-ordinator's expertise.

Support notes for teachers

Spend a little while looking at the examples on pages 40-41 and notice the process. If you think it would have benefits in your school, the challenge is to make the system work. A little time and a few ideas can give a lot of help to every teacher.

The example on page 41 shows support for teachers by an art co-ordinator. The teachers' planning within a topic framework has identified aspects of art within a general theme. The plan is given to the co-ordinator who works on the specifics and offers clear suggestions about content that would fit the focus the teachers are working on. It takes time to do this but it involves the co-ordinator in the planning phase, it represents an aspect of monitoring curriculum provision and it gives a real chance to influence children's learning and classroom practice. If each subject co-ordinator gave this sort of help throughout the school, the spread of teaching and learning opportunities would get wider. The help could be a workshop activity for a school closure day. It may seem that every closure day brings yet more content and further complications to a co-ordinator's work, but by supporting each others' subject planning, co-ordinators can come away with some problems solved, some ideas gained and some ways forward identified.

The example on page 41 shows very specific support notes that can be used within a scheme of work. You could produce practical examples of how to do something, ideas for display, school procedures and sample lessons. The scheme of work does not have to be cumbersome. It needs to be helpful to busy teachers who are grappling with teaching this subject among many others, while coping with the daily challenges of classroom life.

Support notes for the teaching of weaving from 5 to 11 years

In subjects where specific knowledge or experience are required this sort of support is invaluable.

Weaving

Paper weaving using cut strips to practice in/out technique.
Cut strips should be approx 2 cm wide as should loom.

Frame looms - more for the older child.

Crescent loom weaving - the warp should be fairly rigid. Creating the crescent from which the loom gets its name.

Bodkin

Weaving wool and rags is suitable for these looms.

Wool works up faster if doubled or trebled.

Circular looms - another dimension for weaving.

Weaving shapes/holes etc.

Sc 2 Life and Living Processes (Strand 1)
Life Processes and Living Things.

Support offered this way not only provides lots of ideas for starting points for activities, it also provides a stimulus for how the work might be displayed during or after.

Teachers looking at this sort of guidance during planning an activity will also be alerted to the resource implications of it.

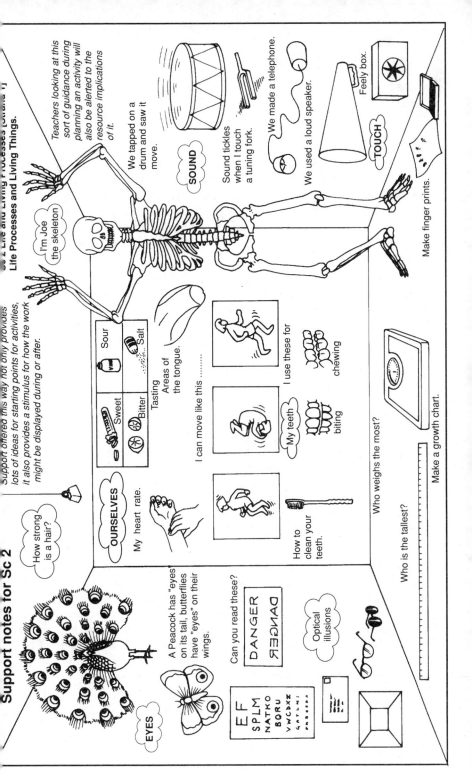

SOUND

We tapped on a drum and saw it move.

Sound tickles when I touch a tuning fork.

We made a telephone.

We used a loud speaker.

TOUCH

Feely box.

Make finger prints.

I'm Joe the skeleton

OURSELVES

How strong is a hair?

My heart rate.

Sweet

Bitter

Sour

Salt

Tasting

Areas of the tongue.

I can move like this ....

How to clean your teeth.

My teeth

biting

I use these for chewing

Who weighs the most?

Who is the tallest?

Make a growth chart.

EYES

A Peacock has "eyes" on its tail, butterflies have "eyes" on their wings.

Can you read these?

DANGER
DANGER

Optical illusions

E F
S P L M
N A T K O
B Q R U
V W C b x z
G A T L N I

41

Working with other co-ordinators and the school management team

The co-ordinator is part of a team responsible for developing the work of the school. The co-ordinator is also part of a team that supports others. This dual role is one of the difficulties of the job. Another is the conflicts that arise when co-ordinators have to ask people who are more senior to them to follow their instructions. However, co-ordinators need to work as part of an overall team and the co-ordination of the curriculum needs to be effectively planned to ensure progress and development for children.

The job of the co-ordinator is too vast to do all at once, so attention must be paid to different parts of the job at different times. In primary schools many co-ordinators try to do all of the job, all at once, all of the time. This can lead to terrific tension: everybody seems to be asking everybody else to do everything and everyone feels snowed under. There is a danger that nobody achieves anything. If co-ordinators are to make the work of the school more manageable and achievable, then much relies on efficient overall co-ordination.

A possible closure day activity

1 In groups of three study a copy of the chart, All Together in Primary Schools *(see page 43)* for about five minutes. It was developed by the head, deputy and senior staff in a school where people were 'getting in each others' way' by sheer enthusiasm, commitment and willingness to work. The chart shows the state of play in curriculum terms in one school. The columns show the teachers, their posts, their areas of responsibility and their salary scales.

2 After studying the chart, the group will start to see some interesting features of the curriculum in this school and questions will start to be raised. For instance, looking at 'Mrs McIver' and English. According to the senior management, assessment and recording are efficient, resources are well deployed, classroom approaches are supported by the teacher and individuals are helped. There is an English INSET programme planned. This is a school where there are no staff guidelines for English yet and people are only working towards them. The overall picture of English looks pretty positive.

All together in primary schools

Name	Post	Responsibility	Staff guidelines: Working party	Prepared	Produced	Available to staff	Implemented	Assessment/recording: Poor	Developing	Efficient	Resources: Disorganised	Catalogued	Well deployed	Classroom approaches: Monitored	Supported	Individual problems to deal with	INSET programme: Plan	Deliver	Follow up	Other
Mrs Boyle	Head SDP					✓														
Mr Williams	Deputy Head	Behaviour/Parent liaison					✓		✓							✓			✓	
Ms Shah	SNS+2	Early years/Maths					✓			✓		✓	✓		✓			✓		
Mrs McIver	SNS+2	KS2 English	✓							✓			✓		✓	✓	✓			
Ms Smith	SNS+1	Assessment and recording				✓		✓			✓			✓						
Mrs Butcher	SNS+1	Humanities	✓					✓			✓									
Miss Jones	SNS+1	Arts		✓				✓			✓			✓						
Ms Patel	SNS+1	Science			✓			✓				✓		✓			✓			
Mrs Liu	SNS	IT				✓			✓				✓		✓			✓		
Mr Moore	SNS	PE		✓					✓				✓		✓		✓			
Ms Long	SNS	Special needs				✓				✓			✓			✓				
Mr Oliver	SNS	RE	✓								✓					✓				

Looking at 'Ms Smith', assessment and recording practice within the school generally is pretty poor, resources are disorganised, classroom approaches are monitored but nothing more, and the INSET programme is non-existent. Yet there are staff guidelines available to everyone. Different subjects and aspects are at different levels and the ticks help to show an overall picture of where curriculum development is at the moment.

3 Still in groups, spend about 30 minutes making notes on:
- Where should the school go next?
- What should be the priorities?
- What should take precedence?
- What are the first stages for overall curriculum development?
- Whose area should move forward quickly?
- Whose area should wait and mark time?

When the 30 minutes are up, one person from each group could visit another group to explain their group's thinking. Final decisions are not essential. It is probable that several groups have the same sorts of ideas. It is the principle rather than the detail that matters. As an example, some suggestions relating to All Together in Primary Schools which were produced by groups are given below.

English:
Needs preparation.

Assessment and recording:
Needs development/cataloguing.

Science
Assessment/recording/Science work together (possible overload). Possible Science INSET on guidelines available to staff.

Special needs:
Staff meeting to implement.

Humanities:
Needs plan for INSET and staff meetings.

Arts:
Needs to proceed, assessment development.

Science:
Next INSET - make available policy document, discuss. Prioritise assessment and resources.

Humanities:
Produce rough document, plan INSET. Develop assessment and recording, organise resources, begin to monitor classroom work.

RE:
Set off. Mr Smith. Staff guidelines.

English:
Documentation to be completed-for INSET day?

Co-ordinating staff efforts

It might be argued that small schools and big schools are different. Their structures and the pressures upon staff may indeed differ but they share a need for thorough and effective co-ordination of the curriculum.

There are many advantages in the whole staff working together to plan the way in which the curriculum should move forward. It is vital to say to some staff that their area needs to move forward quickly, to others that their subject needs time to consolidate, to tick over while attention is given to other aspects of the curriculum. It is not possible to have INSET on everything all the time, or produce staff guidelines for everyone to read all at once, or for everybody to be organising and cataloguing resources, but by structured co-ordination many things can be achieved.

Some teachers who have gone through this process came up with advantages and disadvantages of working in a co-ordinated way.

Advantages

1 Not as much overload.
2 Energies are concentrated on focused areas.
3 Team building opportunities created.
4 Common goals agreed.
5 Morale improves, stress reduced.
6 Resources better deployed.
7 Greater sense of control.
8 Shared sense of direction.
9 Jobs get completed with good end product.
10 Achievements anticipated, made and celebrated.

Disadvantages

1 Resentment and loss of enthusiasm can occur if priority goes to others.
2 A subject can get forgotten.
3 Some people may feel undervalued.
4 Things happen slower.
5 Staff turnover can change priorities.
6 Some areas may get reduced resources.
7 Promotion hopefuls do not relish 'marking time' or consolidating. Employers usually want proof of activity and action.

You could try introducing All Together in Primary Schools into your school. The senior management will need to come together to put ticks in the columns, and after that each teacher can agree or disagree with the ticks. It is important that it is seen as an issue to do with the curriculum and its co-ordination and not with the personalities of the teachers.

A further way to encourage co-ordinators to work together is to ask them what sort of priorities they see for themselves over the next two years (*see page 46*). The Post Holders' Check Sheet can be used to emphasise important aspects of the job for different co-ordinators and to collate the needs of the school generally. Where teachers have more than one subject area, they could fill in separate forms for each area for which they are responsible. That in itself will highlight the pressures upon teachers as they seek to do their co-ordination job. It will become apparent to management teams that teachers are trying to do an enormous amount of co-ordination work, mostly on top of their class teaching commitments.

Post holders' check sheet - I need to ...

Name ....

Subject/Organisational area...

Date in post ....

Permanent/Temporary (delete one)

During the next two years I need to:

	A lot	A little	Not at all	Number of response Total possible	Action needed (lot + little)
Keep up to date in my subject by reading					
Liaise with other phases/schools					
Attend Consortia working groups					
Attend courses in my subject area					
Evaluate staff needs in my area of responsibility					
Demonstrate good practice to a colleague in my classroom					
Disseminate information at Staff Meetings					
Disseminate information at Unit Meetings					
Advise colleagues					
Organise displays to promote my area of responsibility					
Provide INSET at Unit Meetings					
Provide INSET at Staff Conference Days					
Work alongside a named colleague in their classroom					
Help in the induction of new staff					
Train ancillaries/volunteers					
Communicate with parents by sending information home					
Run Parent Workshops/Meetings					
Order and account for stock					
Organise resources					
Organise support staff/ancillaries to assist in my area					
Meet with colleagues to discuss postholder responsibilities/cross curricular links					
Be involved in 'out of school' activities					
Evaluate the success of my work in my area of responsibility					
Write or update a Policy Statement					
Help produce Schemes of Work					

Organise large scale operations in my area of responsibility (please specify)
Undertake other activities (please list)
Please indicate the best time for a particular focus with a number (1=next term, 2=the following term, etc.)

Working in other teachers' classrooms

> 'The first reaction of many class teachers was to offer a group that I could work with outside; in another classroom, the hall, the corridor, the Moon, in fact anywhere that I could not overlook the classroom teacher that worked with children.'
>
> *A co-ordinator*

Working in other teachers' classrooms is an essential aspect of the co-ordinator's role. It is an aspect which is particularly interesting but it is also one which many teachers find daunting. Every teacher knows what it is like to have someone watching them at work in the complex world of the classroom, where many things can go right but even more can go wrong. When it comes to working in another colleague's classroom, teachers can be so sensitive to the situation that they find it difficult to know where to start.

There is no doubt that the classroom is the place where the most powerful impact can be made. However, this impact can be for good or bad depending upon how the situations are handled. The culture of the school is vital. In some schools, colleagues work alongside each other in all sorts of situations in a very positive way but in other schools, teachers find it difficult to enter each others' classrooms.

What are the advantages of working in other teachers' classrooms?

1 To see what's going on
You can see whether children are getting a good curriculum diet and exploring practical issues. You can see whether resources are being used and are adequate. You can also check whether progression is being achieved through the school.

2 To learn from a colleague
You may be the co-ordinator for a subject but a colleague in another classroom could be absolutely superb at all or part of the curriculum area for which you are responsible.

3 To see whether policies are working
If policies are available and known to everyone then co-ordinators should monitor the extent to which they are successful.

4 To help
The good co-ordinator, given the chance, should be prepared to help a colleague as they try to move their practice forward.

5 To build up professional relationships
In good schools, strong professional relationships are evident. Working in colleagues' classrooms enhances professional dialogue.

6 To develop good practice
By working in each others' classrooms, good practice is shared, new techniques are understood, ideas are transferred and colleagues become more confident. You may see different ways of organising classrooms, alternative ideas for resources, new approaches to integration of IT and heightened awareness of differentiation opportunities.

7 To challenge and confront poor practice
If there is poor practice which is contrary to school policy, then it needs to be challenged and confronted. Poor practice can best be addressed where it takes place: in the classroom.

8 A better pupil/teacher ratio
One extra adult in a classroom might give a chance to reduce the pupil/teacher ratio so that children could work in smaller groups with greater adult attention.

9 Time to observe
Watching a colleague gives every teacher a chance to look at themselves and reflect upon their own practice.

10 A chance to ask the obvious
Working in a classroom with a colleague gives co-ordinators a chance to say 'Why do you do that?', 'How did you organise it that way?' When teachers talk in staffrooms, they talk at a distance; when they are in the classroom, they are close to the action and talk about reality.

11 A start of debate
You might find an opportunity to raise essential points with a teacher. There in the classroom, with it all going on around you, is a good time to talk about what really matters.

What strategies or circumstances might there be?

In some schools, there are carefully planned opportunities for colleagues to work in each others' classrooms. In others, it just happens. There are many possibilities, some are better than others.

Planned
Is it possible to plan how the co-ordinators will work in another teacher's classroom? Sometimes it is better for the teacher if it is planned, although this can cause tension.

Ad hoc
Ad hoc arrangements are often more flexible and more comfortable. They are also easier to avoid, easier to forget and easier to let go.

Regular
An opportunity to work alongside a colleague on a regular basis is very valuable. In some schools, a co-ordinator may have a period of five or six weeks when they have a small but specific timetable opportunity to work with a particular colleague. Everybody knows it is going to happen, everybody is prepared but it has to be helped to happen.

Frequent or sustained
The more opportunities there are to work in another colleague's classroom, the more opportunities there are for development. While time is very limited, chances can be taken. For example, an extended period of teaching practice by a fairly experienced student can relieve a class teacher of some of her own timetabled teaching commitments. Over the period of a practice it is possible for the time to slip away, used in all sorts of 'gap-filling' roles. It could be a priority that a proportion of the time is used to offer sustained and frequent support in another colleague's classroom.

For a specific purpose
A teacher feels happy with the subject but not so happy with the organisation, so support could be offered with a fine focus. Assessment might be an issue for one teacher and the time in the classroom could be devoted specifically to that. For another, the issue could be thematic work.

Taking what comes
While 'take it as it comes' approaches can be beneficial, they are often more hope than certainty. Many schools find that, while in theory they work in each others' classrooms, the practice is rather different.

Some ways of working

There are lots of ways of working in another teachers' classroom and they are all of value. It is choosing the appropriate one that moves practice forward.

1 Teach the class
The co-ordinator could teach the class and give the teacher a chance to watch her own children working with somebody else. This is one of the best ways to encourage confidence in a class teacher.

2 Teach a group
It is possible to 'show what you mean' about a subject by taking a small group, working with them and talking the teacher through what has developed.

3 Teach the class so the teacher can take a group

If a teacher is going to have the confidence to try new techniques it is sometimes better if they can work with a small group of children first. If the co-ordinator can take the class while the teacher has a go with a few children, progress can be seen and issues discussed.

4 Organise resources

Time can be spent in the classroom on something as practical as helping a teacher reorganise resources.

5 Observe children at work

Watching children working from Reception to Year 6 can tell you more about progression, teacher expectation, differentiation and continuity of curriculum than anything else.

6 Help with assessment

Many schools have meetings when they look at children's work and do moderation exercises. A key feature of moderation should be to encourage dialogue between teachers about classroom practice. It also gives the chance to talk about assessment within context, which is fundamental.

7 Observe teaching

In this instance the co-ordinator visits, watches and builds up a dialogue with the teacher, or a series of teachers, about aspects of teaching which are influencing the ability of learning within the subject.

8 Demonstrate

Co-ordinators can write policy documents, hold discussions at staff meetings or lead training days, but a powerful way of helping colleagues to try new curriculum development is to demonstrate. It could be a demonstration of practical mathematics, apparatus work in PE or a way of introducing children to orienteering. A demonstration about which teachers can talk later is a worthwhile reason for working in another teacher's classroom.

Talking about what happens

Working in another teacher's classroom will achieve little if what happens is not discussed. Restricting discussion is difficult, but more will be gained if co-ordinators decide which aspects they want to talk about.

Beforehand

Sometimes it is better to talk things through beforehand. For example, if a technique is to be demonstrated it is often better if the watching teacher has some idea of what to expect. Also, if co-ordinators are going to observe children at work it is helpful for the teacher to know what is to be observed.

In the session

It is sometimes possible to talk to colleagues while the session is taking place. At suitable points within a lesson, when children are busy or engaged in some practical work, two colleagues may be able to chat about what has happened or is going to happen next, or how an incident might be built upon.

Afterwards

Most teachers can find plenty to talk about afterwards. It could be a brief chat at the end of the session, a structured discussion later, or a chance for two or three teachers who have been 'visited' to talk together about what has been observed. Incidental chats are fine and can be productive, but structured conversation means that the important points are addressed.

A common agenda?

Should there be a common agenda between the visited teacher and the co-ordinator? For many reasons given above, there should be, but sometimes both partners are happy just to see what happens.

In writing

Sometimes observations should be in writing. If the co-ordinator is taking the role of mentor then it is important that issues are committed to paper and looked at later. Sometimes, though, writing just gets in the way.

Some possible outcomes of working in other teachers' classrooms

There can be many outcomes, some more apparent than others, but where the culture is right there is much to be gained:

1 Greater confidence
2 More teaching skills
3 More awareness of subjects
4 A willingness to take risks
5 Being prepared to help others
6 More open debates in meetings
7 Positive confrontation and challenge.

Qualities needed for development

It is easy to say 'Let's work in each others' classrooms' but it is a very difficult thing to do. Any co-ordinator who is going to work with another colleague needs to display many qualities.

Humility The best teachers know how demanding and difficult classrooms are. They know how the best lessons can fail no matter how much preparation and planning they have done. The best teachers know that sometimes they can teach the worst lessons.

Enthusiasm All teachers respond to enthusiasm. Take some into the classroom with you.

Critical analysis To make the best use of a visit to a colleague's classroom, co-ordinators need to analyse what is going on in a critical way, to question and wonder in a professional sense. These skills can only be acquired by practice. All teachers need the chance to watch classrooms in action and to ask questions.

Effective planning Careful planning is needed if working in other teachers' classrooms is to be successful.

Commitment It will only work if you want it to!

A sense of perspective Some aspects of your curriculum area may be extremely important: an agreed system of record keeping, or organisation of geography or history resources. A teacher who is dealing with an abused child, a severely disruptive child, an outbreak of bullying or a bereavement may not find some of the 'important' things so important. When you are pushing for professional development, you must know how hard to push and when to stop.

Confidence and nerve Both partners need confidence. They also need nerve; nerve to talk about their strengths and weaknesses, to challenge some of the practice that is going on, and to pay a compliment and to accept one.

Managing resources

As a co-ordinator a major part of the job will be the management of resources. In the broadest sense, resources could include people, time, space, money, books, equipment and materials. The effective use of resources is a tangible way to put the principles of your subject into practice:

- Whole school approaches are promoted.
- School aims can be reflected.
- Responsibilities are clarified.
- Limited resources are used to maximum effect.

Auditing resources

It is sensible to start the management of resources by auditing the current situation.

Do you have an up-to-date list of all resources within your area of responsibility?

Creating such a list provides an ideal opportunity to go into other teachers' classrooms. Teachers will often talk about resources in a relaxed way, leading naturally into conversations about teaching and learning styles, assessment or subject-specific difficulties. However, many teachers are very protective about their favourite pieces of equipment, and it can be difficult to find out exactly what exists in school as teachers squirrel away their favourite possessions.

Do all staff know what is available?

Teachers need a list of apparatus, videos, software and books and where they are stored, and to know where consumable materials are kept and what to do about their replacement.

Can all relevant staff use what is available?

Issues for consideration on staff training days can come to light through an audit of staff understanding of how to use equipment and materials. Staff may need more knowledge of complicated computer programs or pieces of technical apparatus in science, or of how to use apparatus in its simplest forms, such as paintbrush techniques, or mathematical equipment, like Unifix or Multilink.

How are resources being used at present
- frequency and effectiveness?

If extensive resources exist but are not being made available to the pupils or are being used poorly, then the subject is hardly being promoted within the curriculum.

Are the resources accessible?

Sometimes storage becomes a big issue. Apparatus is kept in a certain teacher's classroom, maybe because that teacher uses it regularly, but the difficulty of gaining access during lessons inhibits others. This may be a storage issue but could possibly relate to planning ahead so that colleagues can gain access to resources well before they are needed.

What is the condition of the resources?

The upkeep and maintenance of resources are absolutely fundamental. Sometimes resources need renewing. A long-term view of what is needed is an essential part of identifying priorities within school development planning.

Do the resources reflect progression in children's learning?

A walk through the school looking at the type of resources which children are expected to use from Reception through to Year 6 will say much about the expectation of teachers in terms of curriculum achievement. This does not have to be complicated or concerned with complex resources. It can focus on simple things, such as the calibrations on rulers, the quality of scissors or the paintbrushes children are given to work with. The resources that children are offered can enhance or inhibit their progress, and talking as a staff about the expectations for children as their skills develop will raise all sorts of curriculum issues.

Are there any short- or long-term curriculum changes envisaged which might influence the use of resources?

If teachers are being asked to attempt a new curriculum initiative, such as an outdoor perspective within geography or history, integration of IT into their subject teaching or more practical approaches to music making, it is important that their work is supported with adequate equipment and instruments.

Are you aware of resources in other areas of school which may be relevant to your own subject?

There is a danger that, when co-ordinators do their own audit, they fail to relate their needs with those of others. In a primary school, resources in many subjects overlap and staff may need to be aware of a central resource for all subjects which includes many consumables, small pieces of apparatus used by children, and more expensive reference materials such as software or atlases.

What resources are available from outside the school?

Part of the co-ordinator's job is to ensure that outside opportunities are well used. There may be possibilities in a local teachers' centre, local resource collections or a local library that can add to the teaching within your subject. The partner secondary school may be a source of specialist help and advice. A co-ordinator needs to be aware of what is anticipated within the planned teaching so that these outside possibilities are full exploited.

Storage and retrieval

While storage space is at a premium in most schools, it is sensible to try to establish systems that are clearly understood by everyone. Storage should respond to use, so that some store cupboards are for materials that are used regularly, others are for supplementary or replacement materials or things that are needed infrequently. The important thing is that everyone knows where everything is stored.

Co-ordinators should ask themselves some important questions when deciding where to store resources:

1 How often will this resource be used?
2 Who needs to be able to use this resource?
3 Who will be responsible for managing the storage of this resource?
4 Is a catalogue system needed?

Materials that are regularly in use

Some important questions:

1 Can people get it without disturbing a lesson?
2 Can it be reached without moving a lot of other things?
3 Should books or sheets be kept in storage boxes or folders for ease of transport around school?
4 Do you need a system for retrieval? So often material that is in regular use around school cannot be found. This leads to much frustration. It is possible to have a system where the person who borrows something, leaves a note or marker saying where it has gone.

Materials that are made but could be used again

Many teachers work very hard to develop materials that could be used in future. Does the school need a system so that the potential of such materials can be exploited? For example:

- worksheets - how many should be printed?
- review - how often should materials be checked and looked at again? Revise and replace - when?

Leading meetings

For many people the prospect of leading a meeting is daunting. To hold centre stage with the spotlight upon you as colleagues wait to be led into new areas, to debate crucial issues, to argue moot points or to agree or disagree with proposals is a challenge that many of us could do without. Yet meetings are a fact of life, and in many schools they take up a good deal of time, time that many people think is wasted. Sometimes they are right. Why?

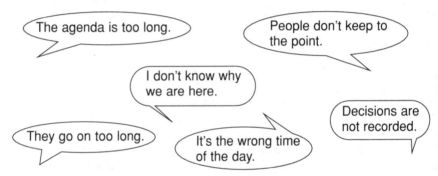

The agenda is too long.

People don't keep to the point.

I don't know why we are here.

They go on too long.

It's the wrong time of the day.

Decisions are not recorded.

Who is responsible for avoiding or dealing with such frustrations? Is it always the chairperson who is at fault? Or does responsibility lie with everyone at the meeting?

Meetings can be helpful. They should:
- bring the school together
- act as a forum for new ideas, decisions, speedy communication and action
- channel efforts into creativity, analysis and problem-solving
- help a team work better together by giving everyone a chance to be involved, making people accountable and letting everyone know what is going on.

Meetings are potentially useful but if the ground rules are not understood and followed they are almost certain to fail.

Knowing why people think some meetings are a waste of time should help co-ordinators think of ways of avoiding many of the problems. The power to do something about the meeting, however, often lies with the very people who make them a waste of time. The chair is often ill-prepared, there is no agenda, people are unclear about the purposes of the meeting and there is little control. It is very hard to do anything about improving meetings, and anyway everyone is too busy doing the real work between meetings!

Lead by example - running a subject meeting

You *can* do something. You could suggest running a meeting, or part of it. A change of approach, even for part of the meeting, might be just what is needed to make people question the way they normally operate - or fail to. If you want your work to be successful, then a meeting can help or hinder; and you might as well use it to help.

Ten tips for success

1 Sort out the timing

How long have you got to say your bit? Sometimes you will have the whole staff meeting, more often you only have a short time within the longer meeting. There should be an agenda for the full meeting and you should try to negotiate with the person preparing the agenda to find the best place for your section. Decisions about a new mathematics scheme are perhaps not best placed between debates about when to hold a bring-and-buy sale and the arrangements for Christmas performances.

It is not good practice to make important decisions at the end of a long meeting. Some people are more interested in going home than in making the correct decision, others are playing for time so that no decision is made and they are not out-voted. The beginning can be the best time, but if there is a really contentious issue to come, the item may not get due attention because people want to get to the big event. Some people use this as a ploy to slip business through in the hope that the implications are not realised by everyone. It might work at the time but only causes resentment later.

It is worth thinking of the complexity of your agenda item:
- If it is easy, idea-sharing and positive then fairly early is fine.
- If it is complicated, difficult and contentious, find a place in the middle, after the easy issues so that people are feeling that things are being achieved when they get to your item.
- If it is short, approval, voting-type business, the end is reasonable, as long as the middle section was not too contentious. At least people feel they are making progress with this sort of item. 'Ideas' items at the end can lead to a lethargic approach as people are tired and mentally switched off.

2 Set the purpose of your agenda

Why do you want to hold a meeting? Does everyone involved know what the meeting is supposed to achieve? It is important to be clear beforehand what you are trying to do. When a group of people sit down to talk with mixed agendas there is confusion, frustration and annoyance. It needs to be made clear whether the people involved in the meeting are expected to:
- offer ideas, suggestions, contributions, thoughts and opinions

- discuss ideas circulated beforehand
- organise an event, materials or programme of activity
- agree and approve plans previously discussed
- plan ways forward, sort out priorities
- listen to information and ask for clarification.

Each of these different purposes should have a very different tone from the others. In a meeting designed to share ideas there should be lots of free thinking, people calling out, perhaps jotting on a chart. In a meeting to agree and approve previous plans there would be more formality, perhaps voting and maybe minutes to record decisions. Minutes would also be used to record the decisions taken when various options are debated but there might be wide-ranging discussion first. Where information is being provided there should be one person talking, everyone else listening, with the person who is in the chair organising questions afterwards.

The purpose of the meeting needs to be made clear to everyone before the meeting, at the very start and at the end. It is just like teaching a group of children: keep explaining what you are trying to do.

3 Sit in a good place

If you want to have impact get there early, find the best place to sit, put your papers on the chair and claim your seat. At some point you are going to have to lead the meeting so sit in a leadership place.

- If the chairs are in a circle then anywhere will do, but any other shape will give problems unless you pick your place carefully. You want a place where you can see and be seen by everyone.
- If it is a long, thin arrangement of chairs, sit at one end rather than on a side. The more you can establish eye contact, the more comfortable you will feel, and the more comfortable and involved your colleagues will feel. You will see people's reactions rather than having to imagine their expressions as you are speaking.
- If you have a choice, sit with your back to a wall rather than the window; your voice will resonate and people will see your expression and not squint at a silhouette.
- If possible, sit so that an interruption at the door is first seen by you rather than everyone else.

All these little things will help you to feel comfortable and confident. Many people shrink away from the front and centre, but because they cannot be seen and heard well, they experience the embarrassment they were trying to avoid.

4 Encourage discussion

You are a few minutes into your talk and you are getting little feedback, there is a silence and you dread asking for questions. Try using groups. Plan to talk for a short time and then ask people to talk in twos or threes before they contribute to the whole meeting. It changes the atmosphere. People can test their opinions, ideas, concerns, worries, on colleagues before committing themselves in front of everyone. There is less likelihood of people fighting their corner for the sake of it, less silence and less hesitance where people dare not say something extreme, negative or positive, in case they get disapproval from others. The tone of the meeting will change if you dare to do it. Groups need only prepare for two or three minutes but they will be minutes well spent.

5 Go boldly through paperwork
If you are running a meeting where you need to talk people through paperwork, plan how you will introduce it. Whatever you do, the minute you give out printed sheets, people will scan them and look right through the document. So take them through it, acquaint them with the route of the document and then come back to the start. If there are sub-headings or bold titles, go through them first; they are like the headlines on the news. Then come back to the text. Explain to the group why you are doing this. Better still, if there is a paper to read, give it out beforehand, ask people to read it and assume they have. If you ask them to read it and then go through it they will not read it next time. Talking through the paper and asking for comments is best done in sections and using groups for two minutes first!

6 Use other people
You do not have to do it on your own. Getting a colleague to help you will remove some of the pressure. A really good ploy is to ask the person who is likely to make you feel most uncomfortable to take notes. They may be so busy writing that they have little time to challenge. The main point is to take the pressure off yourself. In a discussion you need not be able to answer any and every question. You can use others to deflect argument, to bring in people who are generally silent, to add points so far not covered or to check that all the points on a list have been addressed. By using other people you make it a meeting rather than a performance.

7 Think about refreshments
You might have none; it will only be a short meeting. You could have something to nibble before, during or after the meeting. To stop during the meeting is fine but momentum can be lost; the meeting has to be quite long to justify stopping. Refreshments at the end can be useful. People can catch up on personal and professional issues, and the food and drink is relaxing. However, people who are keen to leave can feel trapped by the refreshments laid on.

Many meetings take place straight after school. People are tired anyway, and they are just experiencing a drop in energy as the children leave. To contribute fully to a meeting, they might need a boost. If there are tea and coffee ready as people enter the room, and perhaps some chocolate biscuits, the impact more than justifies the cost and effort. People feel valued, the chocolate gives an energy boost for a little while and because the preparations are made people do not waste time that could be used in the meeting.

Providing refreshments shows that you are in control and are already taking charge of the meeting. If cups start to be collected about three minutes before the start of the meeting, it is a subtle signal that the time is coming for the official business and the tone is set for the meeting.

8 Decide what next
Many meetings fail because, after endless discussion, decisions are not clear to everyone involved. Future meetings are taken up with people clarifying, remembering correctly, disputing, denying, stating categorically, all because a few minutes were not used to state what has been agreed. At the end of a phase of discussion you need to summarise with a clear statement of:
- what has been agreed
- who is going to do what
- by when
- how
- when the issue will be revisited.

It is also worth stating what will be written:
- in minutes if they are usually used
- in notes to all staff if necessary
- in papers to pass round for comment
- to outsiders if necessary.

9 Write to avoid wrongs
Minutes of meetings can be painful, and can ruin the next meeting because everyone argues about the minutes of the last meeting.
A written record can be useful, though. You can use the minutes:
- to clarify who is going to do what
- to record decisions precisely
- to summarise the gist of the discussion
- to avoid confusion over decisions
- to let people who were absent know what happened
- to thank people, indirectly, for their efforts.
The record does not have to be formal, officious or boring. The minutes could be chatty or diagrammatic, have cartoons or charts and pick up the flavour or the purpose of the meeting.

10 Begin and end properly
Whether you are running the whole meeting or just a section, when it is your turn to take responsibility, draw breath and take charge:
- state the purpose, clarify the agenda
- ask for support in your part of the meeting
- present your bit carefully
- record decisions properly
- review agreements and decisions

- restate the purpose of the session
- say thank you; you rely on all the members of the meeting to take responsibility for its success.

Meetings are often ruined because it is getting late. Everyone looks at their watches and shuffles with papers and bags. Less on the agenda, better handled, would make for a better meeting with a more positive outlook.

If meetings are less than effective and you have the nerve to step outside the usual pattern and follow these suggestions, you could be on the way to a successful meeting. Leading a meeting is a demanding task but it can be a positive experience and, because of that, enjoyable and productive.

Planning and presenting an in-service event

Teachers have a lot of experience in planning learning for children. To develop such work with colleagues is an opportunity to extend the skills teachers already possess and add other dimensions to their work. The most common form of in-service event for co-ordinators is the whole staff workshop, either after school or on a closure day. They may also be asked to make a presentation to parents or to talk to governors about the curriculum area. Such events can fill the co-ordinator with dread or excitement. As with all things, planning and preparation will give confidence and help to ensure success.

What is involved in planning the in-service event?

1 Priorities are established in line with school and subject development plans.
2 Purposes are agreed.
3 A programme is planned.
4 Activities are designed.
5 The event is reviewed.

How do I set about planning a training event?

Of course there is no blueprint; everyone has their own preferred ways of working and the people taking part have their preferences for learning. What is actually being planned is a lesson for adults but it is also a working meeting. The skills needed for running an effective meeting (*see Chapter 10*) relate directly to in-service provision.

When you are planning an in-service event, it is useful to ask yourself questions around eight key areas:

- Participants
- Logistics
- Purposes and outcomes
- Content
- Method
- Resources and environment
- Monitoring and evaluation
- Follow-up.

It is much better when there are colleagues to plan with and to support you throughout. The first step, therefore, is to identify one or more colleagues who might help. Then consider each of these eight areas slowly and thoroughly.

1 Participants
The event must be planned with the particular needs of the participants in mind. Some important questions to consider as a planning team might be:

- Who are the participants?

- What are their needs?
- What are their backgrounds?
- Will they be represented in the planning?
- What criteria will be used in selecting participants?
- Do they know each other?
- Who has designed the INSET?
- How can their commitment to the activity be gained?
- How could the threat that some participants might feel be minimised?

2 Logistics

Successful planning will give due consideration to the logistical implications of the event, including time, and financial and human costs. Teachers on in-service courses tend to apply far more rigorous standards to the colleagues who provide these courses than they do to their own management of learning with children. Some questions to consider:

- Who is responsible for identifying needs, organising, financing, designing, delivery, monitoring, evaluating and supporting follow-up for INSET?
- When will the event take place and for how long?
- Where will it take place?
- Are the necessary facilities available (suitably sized rooms, furniture, hardware, refreshments, e.g. coffee/tea on arrival)?
- How many participants will be involved?
- Will staff cover be needed, available, affordable?
- Who will arrange it?
- Are any fees or expenses agreed in writing in advance?

3 Purposes and outcomes

Many meetings and training events fail because there is no clear purpose in evidence. People feel secure when they know what to expect, they can see some sense in it and there are described outcomes. It is essential to state the purposes and outcomes clearly in the course literature, and to reiterate them at the start and end of the event. Some questions to focus on:

- What are the purposes of the event?
- Are they realistic?
- Are the purposes clearly written down?
- Will they be revisited at the beginning and end of the event?
- Do participants understand them?
- What type of verbs have been used in the purposes?
- Will the programme aim to provide understanding/knowledge and action/skills/practice/application of learning to the job?
- Will each activity have a clearly defined objective?

4 Content

Where there are clearly articulated purposes the content is more likely to be perceived as appropriate. However, this is frequently an area where planners and providers fail. Some questions to think about:

- Will the participants see the course as relevant to their needs?
- Is the content consistent with the stated purposes and outcomes?
- Is the content negotiable?
- Will there be any choice?
- Will the course explicitly draw on participants' professional experience?
- Will the course fit into the available time?
- What will be the criteria for deciding who leads the session, given the content?
- Will participants leave the course clear about what they have learned, why they have learned it and how they can use what they have learned?

5 Method

In schools, a balanced curriculum means providing pupils not only with a range of educational experiences, e.g. linguistic, scientific, mathematical, but also with a variety of learning experiences. In classrooms, teachers use a wide range of processes, from talking to the whole group to individual, pair or group work. Sometimes children will sit and listen, read, write, watch, view, discuss, experiment, present or practise. Achieving a balance in the range of activities in a teacher's repertoire makes for a valuable and enjoyable learning experience. The message is obvious for the delivery in INSET.

- What methods would be appropriate?
- Will a variety of activities be used?
- How will balance be achieved?
- Will handouts, transparencies and visual materials be of high quality?
- Will course members be required to undertake any preparatory activity before the programme starts?
- Will the preparatory work be used and valued during the course?
- When will handouts be issued? Why?
- Will participants be actively involved and their experience shared? How?
- Will participants' feedback on method affect future planning?
- Will the method include follow-up?

6 Resources and environment

How many lessons have been unsatisfactory because the appropriate resources were not available at the right time? Teachers will not tolerate inefficiency on courses. Another key to successful INSET is being well organised with your resources. Ask these questions:

- What materials will be needed before, during and after the activity?

- Are a flipchart and stand, video and TV or an OHP and screen needed?
- Are tables needed?
- Where are the power points?
- What happens if the OHP/TV fail? What are the contingencies?
- What will the programme look like?
- What purpose will be served?
- Is/are the room(s) appropriate? Why?
- What messages might they give to participants? Are they tidy?
- What is the best layout of the room for this event?
- Is there enough/too much furniture?
- How will participants be welcomed?

7 Monitoring and evaluation

In school, assessment is an integral part of the curriculum, not a bolt-on appendage to it. This should also be the case with in-service training. Consider these questions:
- What is the purpose of the evaluation?
- Who needs the information and why (e.g. participants, staff development officer, whole staff, governors, parents, trainers, LEA advisers)?
- Who will carry out those tasks?
- What methods will be used to gather data?
- What will be evaluated (e.g. satisfaction, effectiveness, cost, impact)?
- What will happen to the information collected?
- What resources will be needed?
- When and where will evaluation processes be carried out?
- How will this relate to future INSET provision?

8 Follow-up

One of the greatest criticisms of in-service training is that sometimes even the best courses do not result in any tangible enhancement of the provision made for children. The question 'So what?' is important yet infrequently tackled. Here are some specific questions to consider:
- Why is follow-up important?
- When a member of staff returns from a course, what provision is made for a structured, professional conversation about it?
- Whose responsibility is it to ensure this happens?
- What might result from such a conversation?
- What support might be needed for the implementation of planned action?
- Who might need to be informed about the ideas, methods, skills and other messages about the course?
- When is follow-up to occur?

Planning the session

One way to plan the session is to think of it as if you were providing a meal and mirror both the approach and the purposes.

The introduction: appetisers

- An on-screen welcome: music, welcome papers.
- Rapport building: say something to make people feel comfortable, to make them think they are going to have a good time. Show that you are on their side and appreciate their position.
- Purposes, outcomes and approach of the session: by talking about what is going to happen you can limit expectations.
- Equipment and materials that will be available.

The bulk: the main course

The bulk of the session can be taken in any order to suit the purpose and outcome.

- Activities: demonstrate, prove, offer ideas: activities bring the session to life. Participation makes people feel good.
- Show and tell: illustrate points, show a situation, offer data, give practical examples.
- Background: OFSTED, National Curriculum, teacher training agency, research.

Ending : dessert

- Messages: perhaps transparencies, keypoints, practical tips, decisions reached
- Handouts: ready for the end. Giving something to take away, particularly to parents, means that they 'take the school home' and perhaps talk positively with others about the event. For teachers, you want it read; not filed.
- Rapport conclusion: how the session ends will be how people take it outside. Something to end with that sums it up will create the right image. A story, poem, examples from children's work, anything to restate the values of the school within the context of the in-service event.

Personal performance

If the background is thought about carefully using the questions given on pages 62-65 and the session is planned like a meal, the personal performance element becomes less important. That is little comfort for the person who has to do the session, who may suffer stage fright for days beforehand. The truth is that there are no easy answers. Experience helps, tips are useful but in the end it is a case of taking a big breath and having a go.

Some do's and don'ts may help:

Do make sure you have some water available for a dry mouth.

Don't try to learn a script. Put notes on cards and use them as prompts. Try not to read word for word.

Do tell colleagues you are nervous. Ask for some help beforehand, especially from someone you think may be difficult.

Don't hide behind equipment or paper. It is very easy to throw paper around to show how hard you have worked. People do not have time to read it; worse, they feel they could have taken it home rather than join in the session. Try not to run behind the table or OHP and talk across a 'counter'. It makes people feel really uncomfortable.

Do ask people to work in groups to suit the task. Mix the infant and junior teachers up sometimes, or let them work in age groups if appropriate; but you decide and insist.

Don't talk too long. Seven minutes is a good limit. After that people struggle to listen and you get embarrassed at the sound of your own voice.

Do set tapes, TV and OHPs beforehand. It is embarrassing and annoying for everyone when they do not work.

Don't crack jokes unless you are good at it. Jokes could often offend someone in the group, and you need people on your side.

Do try to stand or sit still. Rovers are hard to follow. Try not to fiddle with keys, paper clips, money or earrings. Put them out of reach.

Don't plan too much. Time flies when you are having fun.

Producing a subject development plan

By this stage, you should be aware of the variety of challenges facing a co-ordinator and be able to tease out the issues within your subject in your school. Drawing these together will help you to produce your most important piece of documentation, the subject development plan.

The other documentation connected with the job is useful and important but can develop over a period of time as the school deals with different priorities depending on its stage of development. The subject development plan can be produced at any time as a statement about the state of the subject in the school. It can outline strengths, weaknesses, things going well and things to be developed, such as policy documents and schemes of work. A plan needs to be written regularly, say once a year, and over time it should change to reflect the impact of development, new initiatives and new challenges. It is the documentation that pulls together the strands of the job, sets priorities and keeps things in proportion. It can be done soon after appointment and regularly thereafter.

Purpose

The real purpose of a subject development plan is to provide a periodic review statement about the development of the subject in school. A plan helps other staff see what is envisaged. It helps the management to produce a collated development plan, to prioritise resources and in doing so it strengthens the position of the co-ordinator who has provided an honest picture of the state of the subject in the school.

Two hours to write the plan

Producing the plan need not take long. Two hours of concentrated effort will be plenty. What is needed is a plan which is clear, concise and useful.

Format

A standard format throughout the school is useful. It means that:
- co-ordinators cannot get carried away with their own design and systems
- everyone can read it because they all know the format
- you only have to think about developing the subject, not the way it will be presented
- management can review reasonably quickly the set of subject plans because they can find the same focus

within sections of each plan
- when a new co-ordinator is appointed, the development
  and direction of the subject are charted and understood.

Content

The plan should address key issues that have been mentioned in this
book. It should:
- include the monitoring and evaluation aspects (*see Chapter 3*)
- move forward the audit (*see Chapter 4*)
- bring together stages of subject development, such as the
  production of policy documentation (*see Chapter 5*),
  INSET provision and resource needs.
- state the actions that are considered high priority in the near
  future (*see Chapter 7*), and

The finished plan has to be straightforward and readable. Bullet points
are useful because they state key issues economically.

An example of a development plan produced by a co-ordinator for
geography is given on pages 70-72. It was produced in two hours and,
while it is a first draft, it provides a clear picture of the issues
concerning the subject. Spend a few minutes reading through the plan.
Is it coherent, logical and clear? Does it give a picture of the state of
the subject in the school? Does it outline the future development of the
subject and the best way forward? The co-ordinator found the process
useful and having produced the plan, her confidence in leading the
development of the subject was enhanced. She had a clear direction
and she and others knew where the school needed to go next.

Development plans cannot be written from scratch, the co-ordinator
has to know where the subject stands. After a term in the job, it should
be possible to produce a plan; before that the evidence has to be
gathered. If you feel the format would be useful to you and your
colleagues, you need:

1 Someone to type the headings on to a word processor. If the
   clerical assistance is not available, a governor, a Year 6 pupil,
   someone on a secretarial course or a parent may help.
2 A copy for each co-ordinator.
3 Two hours to sit and think through your subject, either on your
   own or with one other colleague. It is an excellent way to use a
   school in-service day. Everyone involved goes away feeling that
   they have achieved something, and feels more secure because
   they have thought through their subject and know where it is
   going. Some things to avoid when doing the plan:
   - Do not play up strengths or play down weaknesses, or vice
     versa. Make an honest assessment of the subject.
   - Keep statements simple.
   - Do not expect too much. The work must be achievable within
     the context of all the other things that have to be done.

Planning the way forward for your subject

Geography
The Development Plan
(lst draft)

The current situation

The standards of achievement of children are:
- mapping skills noticeably improving - shows in other subject e.g. maths (grid references).
- poor use of geography vocabulary and general knowledge.
- overall satisfactory but awareness that achievement in geography not as high as in other subject areas.

The quality of teaching is:
- good relating to map work and related skills.
- improving on 'themes', but hindered by lack of resources for class/group lessons.
- very good local but contrasting localities unsatisfactory both KS1 and KS2.

The quality of learning is:
- stimulated by displays all around school.
- encouraged in cross-curricular approach.
- generally improving but as co-ordinator, I am aware we need development of schemes of work showing continuity and progression.

Assessment, Recording and Reporting within the subject is:
- continual Teacher Assessment.
- using LEA yellow profiles at least twice a year.
- KS1 use school books.
- KS2 transition from school books to file currently.

Curriculum monitoring through focused audit reveals:
Teachers struggling to deliver curriculum through lack of resources and written guidance from co-ordinator or schemes of work showing appropriate provision/progression.

Specifically, monitoring of aspects of provision raised the following issues:
Learning experiences
- Our school and local area well covered, but neither KS satisfactory in contrasting locality work.
- At present, not addressing all 'themes'.
- Evidence of practical and written work at both KS.
The learning environment
- Nice wall displays both KS, but no reference area for children.
-
-

Resources
- No scheme for KS2 (except Outset Geography).
- Lack of atlases for KS1 and 2. No aerial photos - no money to develop films etc.
- No money to purchase in foreseeable future.

Documentation for the subject is ... developing. A policy has been written but no topic matrix yet which addresses NC requirements fully and thus no scheme of work.

The priorities for the development of ... geography... are:
- topic matrix, having discussed which approach with all staff.
- schemes of work.
- awareness of resources and what outside agencies can provide.
- recording and reporting - useful to new teacher.

Given the time available beyond normal teaching commitment; involvement in whole school initiatives, and supporting other co-ordinators, the development of ...geography... should work to the following plan.

1 Develop a topic matrix approach either
a) timetabled weekly as a subject with own topic/theme,
b) themes to be covered as part of wider topic (e.g. science/history topic) and timetabled as necessary part of topic work,
c) short bursts on a theme/topic lasting 3-4 weeks. (Summer 1995)

2 Write gradually (perhaps term in advance) schemes of work that show progression, e.g. R - our school, KS1 - our village, KS2 - our town. (Begin Autumn 1995)

3 Staff meeting/INSET time to discuss resources, storage and present ideas of recording and reporting. (1995, 1996)

4 Review policy. (1997)

Term 1: Summer 1995

Focus	Task	Involving	Time needed	Completed by	Outcome	Resources needed
Develop topic matrix.	Decide what topics to be covered at both KS and how delivered.	All teachers.	Extended staff meeting approved.	July 1995.	Outline of working document.	NC requirements. Suggested plans to present and use as basis to start discussion.

Term 2: Autumn 1995

Focus	Task	Involving	Time needed	Completed by	Outcome	Resources needed
Begin development of schemes of work (one theme running through school).	Develop work. Evaluate. Modify.	All teachers but need liaison separate KS.	Initial planning in August. Evaluating in December.	On-going.	Working documents continually being revised.	Time.

Term 3: Spring 1995

Focus	Task	Involving	Time needed	Completed by	Outcome	Resources needed
Continue with schemes of work. Co-ordinator to particularly focus on contrasting locality.		Co-ordinator.	Possible INSET course/visit to locality to develop work.	Summer 1996.	Work packs for KS1 and KS2.	Money for supply.

Term 4: Summer 1996

Focus	Task	Involving	Time needed	Completed by	Outcome	Resources needed
Co-ordinator to particularly focus on contrasting locality	Help staff write more meaningful comments.	Co-ordinator.	Possible INSET course/visit to locality to develop work.	Summer 1996.	Work packs for KS1 and KS2.	Money for supply.
Recording and reporting.		All teachers.	Staff meeting or INSET time.	June 1996 (ready for yellow profiles).	To help write yellows.	Examples to present to staff.

Term 5: Autumn 1996

Focus	Task	Involving	Time needed	Completed by	Outcome	Resources needed
Resources.	Increase staff awareness. Central store. SEN children. Prioritise future purchases.	All teachers. SMT	Staff meeting x3 (10 minutes).	Easter 1997.	Better use of existing resources and clear future priorities to purchase.	Time! Money!

Term 6: Spring 1997

Focus	Task	Involving	Time needed	Completed by	Outcome	Resources needed
Resources.	Increase staff awareness. Central store. SEN children. Prioritise future purchases.	All teachers. All teachers.	Staff meeting x3 (10 minutes).	Easter 1997.	Better use of existing resources and clear future priorities to purchase.	Time! Money!

Preparing for the OFSTED inspection

Since the role of the co-ordinator is a vital one for the school, it is clear that the co-ordinator has an important part to play when the school is inspected. The *Guidance on the Inspection of Nursery and Primary Schools* (HMSO, 1995) outlines ways in which the process of inspection is intended to be as helpful as possible for the school. The aim of inspections is to give an accurate picture of the school's performance in terms of:
- the quality of education provided
- the educational standards achieved
- the management and efficiency of the school
- the spiritual, moral, social and cultural education of the pupils.

All teachers are involved in all of these dimensions of the school, and each co-ordinator needs to be aware of their responsibilities and the way their subject influences the overall picture. An inspection is a time for people to work together to provide an overall, rather than a fragmented, picture of the work of their school.

The inspectors' report

The *Framework for the Inspection of Schools* instructs inspectors to produce a clear and readable report. As well as making accurate judgements on 'main findings' about the school, the inspectors should state precisely what needs to be done, the 'key issues for action'. In this way OFSTED intend that the report will be a developmental document for the school.

A report can put the school in context, recognising the influences upon it. The social background of pupils, the state of the buildings and staffing difficulties can be acknowledged as factors influencing the work of the school. The report can make reference to the development of the school, and where appropriate recognise where the school was, is now and plans to be in the future. This helps the school in which significant strides have been taken, but which is not yet where it would want to be. To have an outside confirmation that the school is going in the right direction adds weight to the work of the school and acknowledges achievements made to date.

The inspectors make their judgements on the basis of evidence from different sources:

Observing lessons
In primary schools the inspector can observe the teaching going on in the lesson rather than the subject. Evidence about subjects is collected and reported upon but where the children are working on two subjects within one activity, this can be included in the observation. This recognises the complexity of the primary classroom and the fact that lessons are often not one-subject events.

Talking to teachers about their lessons
Inspectors are asked to hypothesise with teachers about their observations, to ask the teacher's opinion, to check their interpretation of an issue. They still have to make judgements, but the teachers can at least explain their thinking.

Talking to children
Inspectors can talk to children in all sorts of situations: during lessons, around the school, about displays, looking back through books and listening to readers.

Looking at children's work
It is usual for the inspectors to ask to see examples of the work of able, average and less able pupils in each class. This helps them to look at standards, progression, consistency, marking, coverage of subjects and assessment.

Studying teachers' planning
As well as observing planning processes, the inspectors will look at coverage, progression and whether assessment informs planning.

Looking at assessment and record-keeping patterns
The inspectors will want to see if systems are informative, maintained and used.

Studying displays
Children's work will show work covered recently and whether the subject is valued as much as others.

Checking on resources
The inspectors will look to see whether resources are adequate for the work planned in the subject and whether teachers and children can use them. Where there is a central, shared resource, they will want to see whether storage and retrieval systems are efficient.

Studying documentation
The policy (*see Chapter 5*), the scheme of work (*see Chapter 6*) and the curriculum advice (*see Chapter 6, pages 40-41*) all offer the inspectors evidence about the planned provision for the subject. The subject development plan (*see Chapter 12*) puts the work in context. A good development plan is an honest statement of where you are and the inspectors will appreciate and acknowledge the true situation rather than the rhetoric that does not match the reality they see.

Talking to support staff
The inspectors can check on the way curriculum support is deployed. They will want to find out whether people are clear about their roles and whether they are being used effectively. By talking to people involved in classrooms and elsewhere, they will gain impressions of the way they are involved and whether pupils are supported appropriately.

Interviewing co-ordinators
The interview with the co-ordinator draws together the evidence gathered elsewhere and helps the inspector to put issues into context for the report. The prospect of an interview with an inspector can be daunting but it is a real opportunity to make sure that the school's picture of the subject and its development is painted. For the co-ordinator, the interview with the inspector is important. So prepare for it.

Making preparations

The inspectors will appreciate it if you are ready to talk to them about your subject. Through the head teacher, they will negotiate a time for an interview. Some teams provide an agenda for the meeting, others like an open-ended approach. Either way, try to be ready to present your thinking, take a lead, be positive. You might like to suggest, through the head teacher, that you have a meeting early in the inspection to explain the subject, with a further meeting later on to discuss the issues arising. Taking the initiative in this way will help you to be positive and help the inspectors to understand what is really happening within the subject and present a report that is as fair as possible.

If you are going to present a true picture of your subject, there are several things you can do to ensure you do so confidently:

1 Use the structure of this book to assist your preparation
Each chapter covers an aspect of your responsibilities. Be clear about:
- the principles for the teaching of the subject
- how the National Curriculum should be addressed in your school.

2 Collect a box of children's work
This will show how the subject has been addressed over time in different parts of the school. It will help you to show:
- the range of the subject
- links with other curriculum areas
- times when the subject was taken out of school
- times when the subject stands alone
- times when the subject was practical or investigative.
Having collected the box of work it needs to be sorted and labelled so that you can lead the inspector through the collection.

If the inspection team can find no evidence of the subject or only limited coverage during the inspection, it can be reported that coverage takes place as long as it can be demonstrated to the team. An effective way to demonstrate it is to have the children's work available; start collecting now. On each closure day, ask for one hour to sort the box. Everyone will be pleased to see the evidence of how much quality work is being done.

3 Collect examples of teachers' planning

A pack of long-, medium- and short-term planning will help the inspectors to follow things through from the National Curriculum to the classrooms. Try to show evidence of planning at different key stages, in different attainment targets and for different abilities. Make it easy for the inspector; focus attention with judicial use of a highlighter pen so that your conversation is directed and you get confidence from leading the inspector through something you are familiar with and recognise. By doing this you will also show the inspector that you do your job as co-ordinator by keeping a check of teachers' planning processes.

4 A collection of assessment and record keeping

A pack of materials, referenced to children, level descriptions and planning, will serve many purposes. Include provision for children with special needs within this section.

5 Be aware of displays around the school

Walk around the school before the inspection and make sure you know where your subject is represented in display. It could be the main focus or just contributory. While it should not be necessary to 'dress displays up' for the occasion, you might like to try to ensure the subject is represented and that different aspects of it are covered. There are plenty of mathematics displays that include shape but fewer that cover number work. Knowing what is where will show that you understand the subject in school. You could keep a set of photographs of previous displays in your OFSTED box.

6 Know the resource issue

Be prepared to talk about what there is, where there are gaps and what plans there are to fill them. Try to explain the spending policy in the subject and be ready to explain how you know that spending has been well targeted and well used.

7 Show how you monitor and evaluate your subject (*see Chapter 3*)

Show how you know what is going on in your subject and that you know how to prepare an action plan. Inspectors need to see that the co-ordinator is monitoring but they want to know that results are being evaluated and acted upon. They want to be assured that you know the issues and that action has taken place or is planned. They also want to know whether any changes have worked. Be ready to answer the question, 'How do you know it is working?' This is where you need the success criteria, the ways of checking progress in developments.

8 Get documentation tidied up

The paperwork is only one element of the inspection evidence base. It should be genuine, not specially done. It is no good typing out superb documentation that does not reflect the work in the subject. What there is should be tidy and workable, but do not produce guidance that nobody else has seen! If you have a full set, then fine - you can show:

- policy document
- scheme of work
- subject guidelines offering background advice for staff
- booklets for parents
- subject development plan.

If you do not have all of these, the most important one is the subject development plan (*see Chapter 12*). The development plan tells everyone what the state of the subject is, and if a scheme of work is needed then it will say so in the plan. Instead of trying to hide things, the plan explains what is good, what is lacking and when developments are planned. A good development plan puts the co-ordinator in control and is the perfect preparation for inspection. Good planning will be recognised.

9 Network with other co-ordinators

It may be sensible to talk together before the inspection to anticipate issues that the inspection team will question and how you will respond. If you work in pairs to prepare, you will find your confidence grows as you realise how much you have to show the inspectors.

10 Do not panic!

Inspections are stressful. The thought of the press comments afterwards, the possibility of letting colleagues down, the 'being on view', are all threatening to some people. There any many horror stories about what has happened in 'one school I heard about' during an inspection; doubtless there are examples where things have gone wrong for schools, teachers and inspectors. Most inspectors, though, are people who have been very involved in schools and want the school to benefit from the process. Schools where things go wrong are in a minority. There are also many schools that have found the inspectors extremely helpful, highlighting successes as well as constructively identifying areas for improvement. Most teams are very professional and make every effort to allow the school to show itself in the best light. It is so much easier when the school is prepared.

At the end of the inspection

As the inspection finishes, the inspection team will arrange to give feedback to co-ordinators about each subject. If you are responsible for several subjects then the team will try to combine the sessions rather than expecting you to go through a series of feedbacks. The inspector will talk you through the points that will be made in the report and you will be able to respond. Most co-ordinators find this helpful and an interesting outside view on important aspects of school. While the inspector is sharing judgements, there is a clear instruction that advice should not be offered. It is for the school to decide how it moves forward from the inspection findings.

Use the audit of the OFSTED inspection to create an action plan; and use the technique described in Chapter 4 to help you. The OFSTED inspection is an example of an audit carried out by fresh eyes from outside.

Summary of documentation

Action Plan
An Action Plan is a detailed plan addressing one aspect of proposed development.
- It should be done as soon as you can after appointment and reviewed every year.
- It provides a focus for your work.

Policy Document
A Policy Document states principles for the subject.
- It should be done within one year of appointment.

Scheme of Work
A Scheme of Work organises the content of the subject and provides guidance for teachers about methods of teaching.
- It should be done within one year and reviewed yearly.
- It should be flexible enough to include new ideas at any time.

Subject Development Plan
A Subject Development Plan shows the state of the subject at present and a timescale for development.
- It should be produced as necessary.
- It usually has an audit as its first stage.

Index